bQUICK® Coaching

The Fast Track to Lasting Change

bQUICK® Coaching

The Fast Track to Lasting Change

Lisa Brice

Praise for bQUICK® Coaching

The bQUICK® Coaching Model has transformed the way we run our business. The model is quick, effective and versatile. I have personally used it in 1–1 situations with numerous employees and have witnessed immediate huge positive changes. Rolling the bQUICK® Coaching Model out in our business has created a solution-focused culture of coaching throughout that has our employees feeling empowered and valued. This has had a dramatic influence on the business as a whole, from culture to profits.

It is easy to remember and therefore easy to use in any situation that presents itself, be that in the corridor or in a more formal setting.

The book is a great read – quick and easy. The stories bring to life the model and are very relatable to everyday situations in the workplace.

Creating a culture of coaching in a business is no mean feat and the bQUICK® Coaching Model does just that in 90 minutes! We insist that all our management team read the book as part of their onboarding.

I cannot recommend it enough. You can count me as a 'raving fan' of the bQUICK® Coaching Model!
Sam Golden PGDip, BSc Hons, MCSP, MACP; Group Director of Back & Body Clinics

≈

A fresh approach to effective coaching when time is limited. Lisa simplifies the complexities of coaching techniques so they can be understood and applied by all. This is an excellent guide, equipping you with skills that will produce a positive impact beyond your workplace.
Sarah Canning, mediator and solicitor

≈

Take the time to read this book and BQUICK® will pay you back in time and the satisfaction that you have improved relationships whilst getting more out of your team.
Leigh Mann, MD, Piroto Labelling Ltd

≈

This little book offers big riches, with all you need to start having coaching conversations later today, plus nuggets from seasoned coaches' favourite approaches to tempt you to enhance your skills further.
Wendy Sullivan, Clean Language trainer and coach

≈

Well, I wish I had been given this book when I first had team leadership responsibility! The ideas and processes would have helped me no end to learn to be a better leader and coach much more quickly and with better insight.
Joanna Jesson, leader

≈

This little book potentially solves one of the biggest barriers to a coaching leadership style – the 'I don't have time' deflection. The bQUICK® model shows how anyone can start to coach their teams and people right now and the great outcomes that can flow from that change. Insightful and timely.
Nigel Girling CMgr, CCMI, FInstLM; writer and speaker on contemporary leadership issues

≈

A quick read that mirrors the bQUICK® model. This book will transform your life as a leader, manager and even a parent. Lisa has made a potentially complex subject clear, easy to understand and available to everyone.
Jacqueline Harris, executive and outdoor coach, Breath of Fresh Air

≈

Lisa Brice is a truly remarkable coach, combining myriad techniques to create a coaching process that transforms lives. I'm delighted she is sharing bQUICK® with the world, empowering others to develop themselves and their colleagues through this insightful model. This is certainly a model I will be promoting with my clients!
Dr Rona Mackenzie, Director of Youth Leadership, Inspirational Development Group

≈

I found this book an excellent tool in clarifying the difference between coaching, mentoring and training. Simple for any reader to understand and embrace, the model itself elicits an outcome-focused and inclusive modality that all managers will find simple to use, which will enable excellence within their team.
Julia La Garde, NLP coach

≈

What Lisa has done so brilliantly here is to make powerful transformative conversational skills available to everyone. Thanks to this model, we're already seeing a huge impact with our own clients worldwide and in my own practice as an executive coach.
Stephen Manley, accredited executive coach, People Director at Spitfire Consultancy and founder of Inspiraction Coaching

≈

I love the simplicity and accessibility of this book and the bQUICK® Coaching Model – it really can be used by anyone. It contains many golden nuggets and is a great resource you can pick up and access whenever you're looking for a quick prompt or reminder. Another gem from Lisa Brice!
Louise Gordon, change consultant and coach

≈

*To my parents, who gave my sister Anna and me
our love of learning.*

Contents

Part One: Introduction

About This Book

Putting 'coaching' and the instruction to 'bQUICK®' next to each other is, in itself, a bit of an oxymoron. The whole point of coaching is to allow the other person the time and space to think through a situation in order to come up with a solution. Yet here I am, offering you a coaching model that can be done at speed!

Allow me to explain my rationale.

For the last three decades I have dedicated my professional life to the pursuit of coaching excellence. My passion is to facilitate insights and behavioural change that foster transformation and deliver tangible outcomes for my clients, their teams and their businesses.

Over the course of my career, I've come across thousands of time-pressured business people who would love to do more coaching. However, they often resort to adopting a directive 'telling' style of interaction in response to being bombarded with information and the need to constantly juggle priorities.

Perhaps you recognise yourself in what I'm describing.

On the surface, it appears easier and quicker to tell someone what to do – or even just to do it yourself – rather than get into a conversation about it. And because you are experienced in your business, chances are you already know the best approach.

However, you can often find there are consequences to this approach in which you end up in a vicious spiral: your people keep coming back and expecting you to fix all their problems; they lose their creativity and it falls to you to come up with new ideas; finally, somehow, they just don't seem to be solution-focused or accountable for their own performance.

The purpose of this book is to offer you an alternative.

It is to encourage busy business people like you to adopt a coaching style to your conversations; to enable you to develop and empower your people, and cultivate a culture of personal responsibility, accountability, and resourcefulness in your teams. Having a coaching style enables you to lead with curiosity and compassion. Being curious will help you become a flexible leader, enabling you to better navigate the dynamic nature of our fast-moving world.

Thank you for making the time to read this book. It is intended to be a practical guide through an easy coaching process without lots of theoretical or academic models. My hope is that you can follow the structure and implement the techniques really quickly. Anyone can use it – whether you are an experienced coach, new to coaching or never coached before, I'm confident you will find it useful! The invitation is to adopt a coaching style to your communication – asking questions rather than telling someone what to do or allowing your 'Advice Monster' (as Michael Bungay Stanier calls it) to take over.

I purposefully set out to write something that is easily accessible and, in the interests of being quick, I've kept it short. You could probably read this book, cover to cover, in about 90 minutes! If you prefer to take your time and dip in and out, Chapters 1 to 6 can be read in isolation. This would allow you time to implement the practices and integrate the learning before moving onto another chapter that takes your curiosity.

I hope you enjoy reading it and find valuable insights within. My heartfelt desire is that you uncover some golden nuggets of information that you can use to good effect in making a positive difference, both to yourself and those you coach.

About bQUICK® Coaching

bQUICK® Coaching is a 'corridor coaching model'. It gives you a quick, easy and effective way to coach in the moment, anywhere you choose – in a corridor, at a coffee shop or even while sitting at a computer. This model will give you a fast track to lasting change.

Actually, the invitation is to go further.

I strongly believe coaching should not be limited to managers or leaders; rather, it is a collective responsibility. Engaging in peer-to-peer coaching and coaching upwards within a reporting structure significantly contributes to fostering a coaching culture throughout an entire organisation. In doing so, you can cultivate a supportive atmosphere, break down hierarchical barriers, promote collaboration and creativity, and establish psychological safety within teams. Coaching really can become 'the way we do things around here'.

So, how can you initiate a journey in this direction, enabling you to enjoy the rewards of fostering a fully integrated coaching culture and reaping the associated business benefits? In the next chapter, you'll find a comprehensive list of compelling arguments for developing a coaching culture in your business.

Of course, it would brilliant if all your colleagues went through a comprehensive coaching programme and then you implemented formal monthly coaching sessions for everyone at all levels of the business. However, even if you did this (and I'd highly recommend you consider it), you still haven't addressed those conversations where one person asks another person for advice on how to fix a problem.

This is where the bQUICK® Coaching Model sits on the continuum of coaching interventions. Here we have the opportunity to have a focused, coaching-style conversation in a short amount of time – seven minutes or less, often on the move or in an informal setting.

Yes, you might be asking six questions instead of just sharing your wisdom, meaning the conversation might take a couple of minutes longer than previously. In my experience, it is absolutely worth the time investment. Adopting a coaching-style approach will save you so much time in the future.

The bQUICK® Coaching Model is underpinned by robust research and a lifetime's experience of coaching. I considered writing this book without reference to any of the models and theories I've drawn on. However, after a conversation with my book coach, I decided I wanted to share with you the opportunity to tap into some of the wonderful resources I've collected over the years.

So, my approach throughout the book is to make mention of a model or a concept, and then signpost you to the resource pages on my website. Wherever you see a reference number, look for the link to more information at the bottom of the page.

Whilst I'd love to positively impact the quality of conversations that take place all day, every day in businesses across the world, we must be mindful that coaching isn't the solution to every situation. Depending on the context, the competency and experience of the person, the complexity of the issue, and how high the stakes are, you may wish to choose a different approach to reach your desired outcome.

We explore the Situational Leadership® Model in the next chapter; it goes some way towards answering the question: *What might be the right approach, right here, right now?*

I've written this book like a story – a story about a team, a bit like your team, who want to improve the quality of the conversations they are having in their business.

They have started to introduce coaching within their business and are keen to develop a coaching culture. They are using the bQUICK® Coaching Model to encourage a more questioning approach and consultative style to their leadership conversations.

Blaise heads up the team. The team members are Ben, Queenie, Udo, Imogen, Christina and Kao. To help reinforce the model, their names and individual coaching stories match the bQUICK® mnemonic, as you will soon discover.

Each of the team members has a problem with one of the six steps of the bQUICK® Coaching Model. They are coached by a variety of different people using the model to come up with solutions to their particular problem. The exception (and there is always one exception to every rule) is in Chapter 6, where Kao is the coach!

In the next chapter you'll meet the team and hear their discussion about the benefits of adopting a coaching style to their interactions and why they're considering the bQUICK® Coaching Model.

In Part Two, Chapters 1 to 6 are stories of coaching conversations within the team that highlight each of the steps in the model. Chapter 4 overlays the coaching story with a commentary on the stages of the bQUICK® Coaching process.

Part Three then reviews the coaching model and summarises the team's successes.

Each chapter concludes with a summary of the bQUICK® Wins – top tips to help you master that particular step in the process.

I appreciate some of the conversations may appear to be somewhat fanciful. However, this book is intended to be aspirational and to inspire you to apply the techniques shared, so that you too can have conversations that flow as easily.

Enjoy!

Introducing the Team
and the bQUICK® Coaching Model

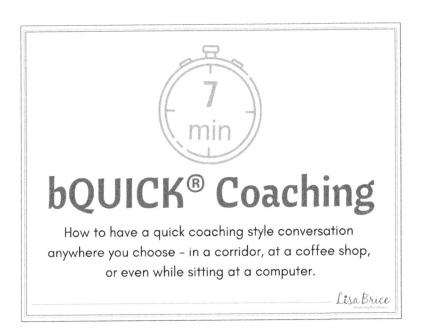

bQUICK® Coaching

How to have a quick coaching style conversation anywhere you choose - in a corridor, at a coffee shop, or even while sitting at a computer.

Lisa Brice

"Business is good – and it could be even better!" Blaise beams as he launches his team's monthly 'Lunch and Learn' session.

"We have seen that introducing coaching to our leadership team has made a dramatic improvement in the company's performance," he continues. "We've received amazing feedback all round; our recent company engagement survey and your individual 360° appraisals show that team morale is at an all-time high. Our quarterly customer insight survey details how customer satisfaction has increased, and our recommendations and repeat business are both up. Our turnover has skyrocketed and all our revenue streams are now profitable!

"I believe we are very much on the right track. I'm really

proud of what we have achieved together. Well done to you –
and please pass on our appreciation to your teams."

There is palpable excitement in the room. Blaise, smiling at
his team, brings up his first slide.

"I want us to build on our successes by embedding a
coaching culture throughout the whole business. We've
already started to witness some of the benefits listed in this
graphic."

The Business Case for Coaching

- Empowers your people, increases employee engagement and improves team morale
- Fosters a culture of personal responsibility, accountability and resourcefulness
- Enhances problem solving and creativity
- Helps create clarity and reduces overwhelm
- Builds rapport and enhances working relationships
- Develops your people and unlocks more of their potential
- Frees up your time to ensure you deliver maximum impact
- Stops the constant need to hand-hold and tell people what to do
- Enables you to lead with curiosity and compassion
- Increases performance and productivity

bQUICK® Coaching   *Lisa Brice*

Blaise continues. "I believe that by supporting our team
members' personal development and growth even more, we
will enhance our already high performing teams. And we can
do this by introducing and encouraging everyone throughout
our business to have coaching-style conversations." He
gestures to open the floor for questions and comments.

Queenie is the first to speak. She lets out a big sigh. "It
sounds great in principle, and I'd love it if I could get my team
to stop bombarding me with questions. Then maybe I could

get on and do my job instead of doing most of theirs for them. That would be a miracle! But I don't have anywhere near enough time to coach everyone. And I doubt they'd ever coach each other."

Blaise responds. "Yes. Before, I might have agreed with you. Finding time to coach everyone has been challenging in the past. We've struggled with how fast the business moves, and we haven't always been able to make the time for formal coaching sessions for everyone. I also appreciate we've talked about the benefits of coaching before and we all recognise the value of it. We've already agreed we want to develop more of a culture of creativity, accountability and responsibility within our teams.

"That's why I'm so excited to hand over to Kao to introduce you to bQUICK® Coaching, which gives us a quick, easy and effective way to coach in the moment. It will enable us to expand a coaching culture throughout the business, empowering our colleagues to be the best they can be."

Kao smiles. "Thanks, Blaise. I recently attended a fantastic four-day coaching programme. I was blown away by the whole experience; it was life-changing!

I'd say it was the best training I've ever had. It was brilliantly delivered, with inspirational content, great food and a fabulous bunch of people, all held in an amazing learning environment. If you get the opportunity, I'd recommend you sign up for it too.

"One of the highlights of the course was learning about the bQUICK® Coaching Model. I was really inspired by how effective it was and how easy it is to follow. I'm really keen to share it with you all today. I agree with Blaise that by growing our coaching culture throughout the business we will reap significant benefits and have an even more engaged and productive workforce."

He looks around the room and sees people looking

intrigued. "Has anyone heard the expression 'corridor coaching'?" he asks. Some of the team shake their heads.

Imogen looks up, a little nervously. "Is it about having a short coaching conversation in the moment?"

Kao nods appreciatively. "Yes, absolutely, Imogen. And the bQUICK® Coaching Model makes it easy for you to have these quick coaching-style conversations anywhere you choose – in a corridor, at a coffee shop or even while sitting at a computer. I believe using this model could be really transformational for everyone. It will enable us to empower our teams to think even more creatively and strategically when finding solutions to difficult challenges."

Kao can feel the energy in the room rising and is thrilled. "This model is an excellent addition to our leadership and communication toolkit. With this in hand, we now have the choice to either direct, support, coach or delegate, depending on what's appropriate for the situation. It will give you increased flexibility to operate in any of the quadrants of the Situational Leadership® Model[1]. bQUICK® Coaching will negate the common worry that coaching is going to take longer than the other options."

Udo smiles. "This sounds really interesting because I do generally worry that coaching will take too long. I often get fixated on the problem and, in an attempt to help solve it, I end up just telling people what to do, which rarely feels satisfying. As a management team, I think our performance as leaders is impacted because we are exhausted by constantly problem solving for our team members."

Kao is starting to relax and enjoy himself. He can sense the interest and growing appetite in the room. "bQUICK®

---

1 For more information about The Business Case for Coaching, Situational Leadership® Model and the bQUICK® Coaching Model, go to www.LisaBrice.co.uk/bquickcoachingresources.

Coaching was originally designed to bring a coaching-style dialogue to any interaction. That being said, it is a fantastic structure for us to use for formal or longer coaching sessions too. We are confident that adding short opportunistic coaching exchanges alongside the more formal coaching sessions we already offer will be an awesome way to implement a coaching culture. And it will really help embed coaching as 'the way we do things around here'."

He looks around the room and sees nods and smiles from everyone. "And the great news is that bQUICK® is a mnemonic, so it is really easy for you to remember the process."

The bQUICK® Coaching Model

b - be Present
- Stop
- Get present
- Connect and build rapport
- Give your full attention to the other person

Q - Question the Situation
- Where are you now?
- Tell me a bit more about ...
- What else ...?
- Is there anything else that would be useful for me to know about ...?

U - Understand the Outcome
- What would you like to have happen?
- And when ...., then what happens?
- And when ...., what does that do for you/get you?
- What aspects of the outcome are within your control?

bQUICK® Coaching

Lisa Brice

The bQUICK® Coaching Model

I - Investigate the Solution
- What have you tried/thought of so far?
- What could you do?
- What else could you do/is there anything else?
- And out of all these solutions, which one are you most drawn to?

C - Conclude the Action
- What are you going to do?
- What might be a good first step?
- On a scale of 1-10, how committed are you to this?

K - Keep in Touch
- When shall we check back in?
- Let me know if there is anything else I can do to support you.
- Is this an OK place to leave this?

bQUICK® Coaching   ———————————   *Lisa Brice*

Kao is keen to get the team's thoughts and see if there are any questions. He looks enquiringly around the room and asks, "What are your views now you've heard about it?"

Imogen smiles and lets out a breath. "I'm up for trying anything that improves relationships and teamwork. And I can easily imagine this working."

Queenie nods in agreement and raises her hand. "It does seem simple to remember. But I bet it takes ages to do – and we never have enough time."

Not wanting to appear abrupt or disrespectful, Kao softens his tone to acknowledge Queenie's concern. "I can see how you might think that, and one of the great things is that the bQUICK® Coaching process can be completed in only seven minutes!"

Queenie raises both eyebrows in surprise. "Only seven minutes! OK, now you have my attention!" Laughing to herself, she says, "Ah, OK, I guess the clue is in the title!"

Kao is keen to hear from everyone, so he stays silent for a

moment or two, making eye contact around the room.
Christina seems a little hesitant. "It's all very well for you –
you've just come off a four-day coaching course. Please could
you give us a few tips on how to use it?"

"Yes, of course, Christina," Kao says. "I'll go through the next
couple of slides and hopefully they will give you a few tips. And
I'll come back to you afterwards and see if there is anything
else you are still unsure about or want to know. Is that OK with
you?"

Christina nods. "Thanks."

Kao smiles back at Christina before he continues. "I really
want to stress that anyone can use the bQUICK® Coaching
Model. You don't have to be a coach. So, here are a few key
reminders about what's important in a coaching
conversation."

What's Important when bQUICK® Coaching?

- Be present.
- Take a partnership approach.
- Build rapport and connection.
- Mirror the person's energy, body language, pace, and voice tonality.
- Focus your attention on the person.
- Listen carefully and let the person do the bulk of the talking.
- Ask questions with genuine curiosity.
- Let the person come up with their solutions.
- Avoid giving advice; your role is to facilitate their thinking.
- Summarise your understanding often.
- Give the person time to reflect and make their own choices.
- Have the person commit to their next step.
- Agree when and how to check back in.

bQUICK® Coaching

Lisa Brice

Imogen smiles at Kao and says, "Seeing all your bullet points
reminds me how vital they all are to having a successful

coaching session, and how different it is from any other type of conversation. And it reminds me how easy it is to forget to do some of them. Please can I have a copy of your slides? They make great coaching checklists."

Christina says, "Yeah, I'd like a copy too. All your tips make sense to me. And I'm reflecting on when I've been coached before, what a rare gift it was to be given time and space to think for a moment. When I am given time, I can come up with a solution that fits my way of working much better than if I'm told what to do."

Queenie chips in. "It's all very well giving people the time and space to think but it is often much quicker for me to direct them, especially when I already know the answer. So there is often no point in coaching them. I can just tell them what to do or, if they are competent enough to handle the task, I can delegate it to them."

"Yes, Queenie," Kao says, "we are not saying that coaching is the best option in every situation. As I said before, this model is an excellent addition to our leadership and communication toolkit. bQUICK® Coaching will now give you more times when coaching is an option for you, so you may well need to rely on directing, supporting and delegating less often."

He continues. "I believe we will we get an even better result when we are delegating or supporting if we have a coaching-style approach. And absolutely, Queenie, sometimes we have to be honest with ourselves and admit that we don't have the time or capacity to coach, or it isn't appropriate to coach. My next slide gives us some useful questions to ask ourselves to determine if it is a good time to coach or not."

Is it a Good Time to Coach?

- Is coaching the most appropriate intervention?
- Is the environment conducive to coaching?
- What are the time constraints?
- How much time do each of you have?
- What is the quality of your relationship in this moment?
- Have you enough information to approach the subject?
- Do you have 'charge' around the person or subject?
- What is your emotional state?
- What do you sense their emotional state is?
- How receptive to coaching do you think they are likely to be?
- Is this the best time to have the conversation?

bQUICK® Coaching

Lisa Brice

Ben raises his hand. "If coaching isn't the most appropriate intervention, what else might be?"

"Great question, Ben," Kao says. "We have already covered that directing, supporting and delegating are all important and vital leadership interventions. So, these are all good examples. And sometimes people might need a different type of support in the form of mentoring, training or even counselling. Obviously mentoring and training are part of what we can offer as managers, but counselling definitely isn't."

Ben nods. "OK, so what's the difference between coaching, mentoring and counselling then?"

Kao responds, "Who would like to share with Ben what the differences are?"

Udo raises his hand. "I can. I actually have a mentor; she's great. The questions she asks really help me think things through. And she's happy to share her knowledge and expertise, as well as give me advice when needed. I guess training is about teaching someone something, whereas counselling is akin to therapy. Coaching is more about raising awareness and helping someone to learn or discover something for themselves, I think?" He looks questioningly at Kao.

Kao grins at him. "Absolutely, Udo. In essence, a coach is someone who helps another person achieve higher effectiveness by creating a dialogue that leads to awareness and action. The coach asks powerful questions, listens carefully to the response, and then reflects back what they've heard. This helps the person being coached to clarify their thinking. Coaching is about bringing out the potential of the person being coached, supporting them as they move from where they are to where they want to be, and acting as an accountability partner through the process. In a nutshell, coaching is really just having a conversation with a purpose."

Everyone nods in agreement.

Kao emphasises the importance of being discerning about time and not settling for a 'half in – half out' mindset. "If you're approached by someone who asks if you have a minute, be decisive. You've got two choices: either make a positive commitment to the person and give them your full attention, or be honest, let them know they are important to you, and say now isn't the right time for you. Then arrange a time that will work for both of you. Is there anything else anyone wants to ask?"

"Actually, I have a question," asks Udo. "In the slide, where it says 'Do you have 'charge' around the person or subject?', what do you mean by 'charge'?"

Kao smiles. "Good question. My understanding is that 'charge' is where we feel a strong emotion that could cloud our thinking. For example, if we felt a 'charge' – say, frustration – in response to receiving an email, we would hopefully type a draft response, wait until we had calmed down before re-

reading, possibly amend it, and then send it. Does that answer your question?"

Udo gives him the thumbs up.

"Any other questions or comments?" Kao enquires. He looks specifically at Christina, who shakes her head.

Imogen speaks up. "I really like the idea of using bQUICK® Coaching. It looks pretty straightforward to me."

Queenie shakes her head. "I guess it's worth a try."

"It sounds great to me," Ben says.

Kao sees the rest of the team nodding and smiling and takes this as a good sign to move on. "Is there anything you'd like to add before I wrap up, Blaise?"

Blaise responds, "Yes, actually there is. I've found an easy way to remember bQUICK® Coaching is to distil it into six great questions:

o   Am I present?
o   What is happening now?
o   What would you like to have happen?
o   What could you do?
o   What are you going to do?
o   When shall we check back in?

"It really can be that simple!

"And I want to reinforce that anyone can coach anyone – you don't have to be a manager or a leader to coach. It's about adding a coaching style to your communication; asking questions rather than telling someone what to do or allowing your 'Advice Monster' to take over.

"I'd love us to cascade and embed a coaching-style approach throughout the organisation."

Wrapping up, Kao is keen to get a commitment. "Does anyone have any final questions before we agree what we are going to commit to as a team? And, if not, what next?"

The team shake their heads and smile. Imogen says, "I think it would be fantastic if we all agree to make a concerted effort to use bQUICK® Coaching as often as possible. We can test it out and report back on our progress at our next team meeting in two months' time."

Delighted, Kao says, "I couldn't have said it better myself! Are we all agreed?"

The team members all murmur their agreement. They seem genuinely excited about the prospect of having short, impactful coaching-style conversations and practising using bQUICK® Coaching.

As each of them leave the meeting, they thank Kao and Blaise for their presentation.

Part Two:
bQUICK® Coaching

Chapter 1: Be Present

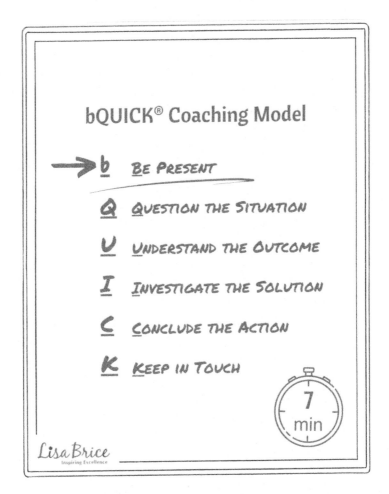

bQUICK® Coaching Model

→ **b**   BE PRESENT

Q   QUESTION THE SITUATION

U   UNDERSTAND THE OUTCOME

I   INVESTIGATE THE SOLUTION

C   CONCLUDE THE ACTION

K   KEEP IN TOUCH

7 min

Lisa Brice
Inspiring Excellence

Ben is walking down the corridor heading to his office when he sees Blaise, his manager. "Hey Blaise, do you have a moment? I wanted to have a quick word if that's OK?"

Blaise is striding to a meeting and has his head down. He looks up at Ben and smiles. "Of course! I've got a maximum of 10 minutes before my next meeting. Is that going to be long enough?"

Ben thinks to himself how lucky he is to have such an approachable boss. "Yes, it's only quick."

Blaise wants Ben to know that he is important to him. "Let's walk together to my next meeting and we can talk on the way. That way, I can give you as much of my time as possible. I'm sure we can make progress in that time! Also, walking often stimulates our creativity and ability to think about things differently. What's up?"

Ben says, "Good idea, that way we maximise our time together. I've been experimenting with the bQUICK® Coaching Model and it has flagged up an issue for me. I'm really struggling to keep my attention in the here and now."

Blaise takes a moment and matches Ben's breathing pattern for a couple of breaths. This helps him focus all his attention on Ben and he starts to build a non-verbal connection. To build even more rapport, he smiles at Ben and says, "How's that daughter of yours getting on at her new nursery?"

Ben smiles back. "Pretty good, thanks! Molly and I are really proud of how she's getting on and particularly how well she is mixing with the other children."

Blaise responds, "That's brilliant, I'm really pleased for you all. So, tell me a little bit about what's going on for you?"

Ben takes a deep breath. "I'm really conscious that I'm struggling to stay focused on the present and not let my mind wander when I'm coaching or in a one-to-one review. I'm also noticing that this happens when I'm in meetings. The other day, when we had our finance meeting, I found myself thinking about how we performed last year instead of focusing on this year's budget and targets."

Blaise nods. "And what else are you noticing?"

Ben frowns, scratches his head and gives an embarrassed laugh. "Well, I'm struggling to stay present at home too. Last night Molly was telling me about her day and my mind drifted off to an email I needed to write. You can imagine that didn't go down well!"

Blaise smiles at Ben. "Yep, I can imagine. And is there anything else about all of this?"

Ben shakes his head. "Nope, I think that's about it."

Blaise pauses and then asks slowly, "And what would you like to have happen?"

Ben considers the question and then responds with conviction, "I'd love to be able to keep all my attention on the person who is speaking, instead of my mind drifting off somewhere else."

Matching Ben's tonality, Blaise probes a little deeper. "And when you keep all your attention on the person, then what happens?"

They both stop walking, and Ben says, "I listen much better and can appreciate more of what they are saying, and indeed what they aren't saying."

"And when you are listening better, what does that get you?" Blaise enquires.

Ben takes a moment and really thinks about the question. "More rapport and a better understanding of what's actually going on."

Blaise reconfirms, "So, you are listening better, with more rapport and a better understanding of what is going on. And is it within your control to put all your attention on the person who's speaking?"

Nodding, Ben says, "Yes, I guess it is."

Blaise wants to empower Ben to come up with his own solution to the issue. "I respect your intelligence, Ben. What have you tried or thought about in order to stay present?"

Ben starts moving again, as he has often found that walking helps him think.

"What's worked for me before is when I really focus on the person, paying attention to their body language and the minute details of their facial expressions. So, building on that, what I could do is notice their breathing pattern and try and match it with my own. That would really help me concentrate on the other person and stay present."[2]

Blaise is conscious not to interrupt Ben's flow. "Mmm, that sounds good."

Ben continues, "And I could also focus on building a connection with them. Taking a genuine interest and finding what they are saying totally fascinating. Rather than jumping in with my questions, I'll be actively listening."

Blaise nods. "Yep, you could do that."

Ben is on a roll now. "Oh, and I remember a friend of mine, a semi-professional rugby player, saying that he was taught to set up an anchor[3], a little non-verbal cue, that he could fire just before he went for a conversion. It meant he could shut everything out, quieten the voice in his head and bring his total focus to kicking the ball and scoring."

Blaise keeps digging. "And is there anything else you could do?"

Ben takes a moment. "I'm not sure."

Blaise doesn't want to put ideas into Ben's head, so he just nods at him encouragingly. "Mmm."

"Well, Molly has been trying to get me to meditate with her," Ben says. "I like the idea, but I find it really hard. Didn't you go on some sort of programme to learn about mindfulness?"

Blaise responds, "Sort of – I went on a HeartMath® programme[4]. The process is kind of meditative but it can be done quickly on the go. It focuses your attention inward, to the heart and onto the breath, and then you recall a positive

2 For more information about Matching and Mirroring...
3 For more information about Anchoring....
4 For more information about HeartMath®...
go to www.LisaBrice.co.uk/bquickcoachingresources.

emotional memory. The process allows you to access a peak performance state by learning to take control of your autonomic nervous system and shifting the hormonal balance for two key hormones in your body – HeartMath® calls it 'Coherence'. This optimal state is when the heart, mind and emotions operate in sync and are balanced. When you are coherent, you increase your capacity to be fully present and are energetically centred, increasing mental and emotional flexibility. There is even a bit of technology you can use to monitor your state of coherence."

"Wow, I like the sound of that," Ben says.

"Yep, the HeartMath® system is pretty cool." Blaise grins. "When I first heard about it, I couldn't believe I hadn't learnt about it sooner. I think they should teach it in schools! So, you've come up with some good ideas about how to get focused on the here and now, Ben. Which one are you most drawn to experimenting with first?"

Ben replies instantly. "I want to learn how to do this HeartMath® practice!"

Blaise decides to take off his metaphorical coaching hat to make a suggestion. "I could tell you the steps now. However, I want to be on time for my meeting and don't want to rush through it. I'm going to suggest you speak to Sarah; she heads up our operations division in the Midlands and I think you've met her before. She is a HeartMath® certified coach."

Ben furrows his brow as he recollects who Sarah is. "OK, yes, I know who she is. I'll ping her an email and see if she can spare me a little bit of time."

They have arrived outside the meeting room and Blaise says, "Great. When shall we check back in so you can update me on how you are getting on? Is there anything else I can do to support you?"

"Nope – I'm good thanks," Ben replies. "Catching up next week would be great – perhaps after our team meeting?"

They shake hands. Blaise enters the meeting room and Ben heads off back to his office.

Next week arrives. After the team meeting, Blaise asks Ben for a quick catch up. "Ben, I'm curious to hear how you've got on with your coherence practice and remaining present with people."

"Well, Blaise, Sarah was fantastic and I've loved practising the HeartMath® technique. I've even shared the Quick Coherence® Technique[5] with some of my colleagues."

Blaise smiles to himself and wonders if he will get away with pushing Ben to talk it through. He decides to go for it. "Go on then, remind me of the steps!"

Ben sighs to himself, knowing he isn't going to get away without proving he knows what he is talking about. He considers pushing back and refusing, and then decides to take the plunge.

"Focus your attention in the area of the heart. Imagine your breath is flowing in and out of your heart or chest area, breathing a little slower and deeper than usual. Find an easy rhythm that's comfortable. I count in for four and out for four.

"As you continue heart-focused breathing, make a sincere attempt to experience a regenerative feeling, such as appreciation or care for someone or something in your life. I try to re-experience the feeling I have for someone I love – a pet, a special place, an accomplishment, etc. – or I focus on a feeling of calm or ease.

"It is easy to remember and really helps me in the moment: all I need to do to get present is heart-focused breathing and activate a positive or renewing feeling."

Blaise is delighted that Ben can recite the technique so fluently. "Well done, Ben. That's how I remember it too. How

---

5 For more information about HeartMath Quick Coherence® Technique, go to www.LisaBrice.co.uk/bquickcoachingresources.

has your HeartMath® practice helped you to be present, more often?"

Ben thinks for a moment. "Well, I can't say that it is easy, but I feel I'm making progress. The other day, I had a particularly challenging performance review with Mary. She was behind on her targets, and I knew I needed to have quite a tough conversation. As you know, our communication styles often lead to tension and sometimes even conflict.

"I'd prepared thoroughly for the review. I organised a room, which was totally private, and we both booked plenty of time in our diaries. Before she came in, I practiced the Quick Coherence® Technique. When she arrived, I deliberately took the time to breathe deeply myself, and then discreetly matched her breathing pattern and some of her non-verbal behaviours.

"I probably spent the first five to ten minutes building a connection and rapport with her. Whilst there were some tough messages to be said, she responded really well and since then I feel we are relating better.

"I know being present is a skill that I need to practise and I'm glad to have a major success under my belt. Since my conversation with Mary went so well, and much better than it would have in the past, I'm feeling more confident. I'm noticing the more present I am, the more presence I seem to have, and the more people are naturally listening to me; it's a bit strange really.

"I used to believe that successful people thought of lots of things all at the same time, and now I'm starting to realise the benefits of just pausing for a moment and connecting with someone. I'm becoming a significantly more present person. I seem to be having greater impact in my messaging, and other people are more engaged and prepared to hear me out – a bit of a win-win!"

Blaise is delighted. "Well, Ben, what can I say? It seems

you've made some great progress. Congratulations and keep up the good work. Please keep me posted on how you get on."

Ben heads off to lunch feeling pleased with his performance and motivated to keep developing his ability to be in the here and now.

Blaise is pleasantly surprised at the profound effect that simply asking Ben a few questions has had. Being present has dramatically improved Ben's communication style and working relationships and, therefore, the team's performance.

bQUICK® Wins:

Be Present and Avoid Getting Distracted

- Use HeartMath's Quick Coherence® Technique to prepare for an interaction and to reset after a stressful conversation.

- Focus on the other person's body language and facial expressions; pay attention to how they breathe and match your breathing pattern with theirs.

- Build a connection by taking a genuine interest in the other person.

- When you first meet someone, deliberately pause and use an anchor to get present.

Chapter 2: Question the Situation

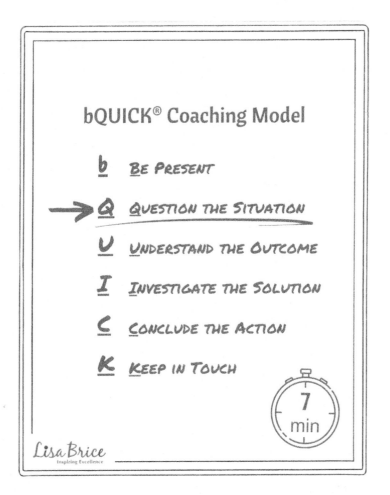

bQUICK® Coaching Model

b BE PRESENT

→ **Q** QUESTION THE SITUATION

U UNDERSTAND THE OUTCOME

I INVESTIGATE THE SOLUTION

C CONCLUDE THE ACTION

K KEEP IN TOUCH

7 min

Lisa Brice
Inspiring Excellence

In desperation, Queenie rings her colleague Quinn and asks if they can meet for a quick coffee. He agrees. They settle into comfy chairs in a secluded corner of the coffee lounge, each with a steaming cappuccino.

Queenie smooths down her new skirt whilst taking a moment to admire the striking pattern. "Thanks for agreeing to meet with me, Quinn. I really appreciate this. I know you're busy and I promise I'll only talk for as long as it takes for you to finish your coffee."

Quinn smiles at Queenie. They've been colleagues for some time now and he's used to these impromptu informal chats. "No worries, what's up? You know I'm always happy to listen."

Queenie grins at him. "Well, you know I told you a couple of weeks ago that we had this big project going on. It was all going great and now it seems to have hit a bit of a stumbling block. I'm totally frustrated. As far as I'm concerned, it's blatantly obvious what needs to happen – any idiot could see what the problem is – and I don't understand why people aren't just fixing it."

Quinn nods and takes a moment. Not only are they colleagues, they are also good friends and have been bantering together for years. Quinn knows he can be provocative with Queenie. "Ah, this old chestnut again."

Queenie pretends to be shocked. "What do you mean?"

"What do you think I mean?" Quinn fires back.

Queenie lets out a sigh and thinks to herself, "Good old Quinn, he's called me out again!" She says out loud, "That I'm jumping to conclusions again and getting all judgemental about the situation without doing any investigation!"

Quinn does a good impression of looking stern. "Yep, pretty much. And what else?"

Queenie becomes serious and looks him directly in the eye. "I'm not asking any questions about what's going on. Nor am I asking if they can even see the blockage in the workflow. I'm just getting impatient and being really directive – and, although I hate to admit it, perhaps a bit manipulative."

Quinn enquires, "And is there anything else about all this?"

Queenie considers the question. "Nope, I think that's about it."

Quinn knows Queenie likes to work at pace and decides to

move on to exploring the outcome she wants. "And what would you like to have happen?"

Queenie comes straight back. "I'd like them to blooming well hurry up and sort it out."

"Yes, and what could the development opportunity be for you?" Quinn challenges.

Queenie appreciates she is being pushed and knows Quinn won't back down. "Ah, I see where you're heading with this. I could have a go at flexing my style by asking more questions and seeing what solutions emerge. This is an opportunity for me to test out what happens when I get curious and adopt a more collaborative approach, as opposed to my typical directive 'telling style'."

Continuing to push, Quinn asks, "And when you are being more curious and collaborative, what does that get you?"

Queenie leans back in her chair. "Well, I'm more likely to keep the project team engaged. And perhaps – and it's a big perhaps – they might come up with an idea that I haven't thought of!"

Quinn keeps going. "And is it within your control to be more collaborative and ask more questions?"

Queenie smiles to herself. She really loves the challenge. "Of course it is."

Quinn is always impressed with how resourceful Queenie is. "This isn't the first time we've talked about how you could be more collaborative. I remember in the past you've tried a few things that seemed to work well for you. Which of those might be helpful in this situation?"

Queenie's breathing slows down as she considers what's previously been successful for her. "One of the things I tried before was to make myself ask at least three open questions[6]

---

6 For more information about Open Questions, go to
www.LisaBrice.co.uk/bquickcoachingresources.

before I gave my opinion. And, thinking about it, one of the things that seemed to work really well was when I used 'how' questions instead of 'why' questions."

Quinn is loving the dance in their conversation. "How do you mean?"

Winking, Queenie exclaims, "Ooh, clever – just like that!" She carries on. "I've found asking 'I'm curious about how you chose to approach it in that way' gets a much better response than 'Why did you do that?' I think it's because a 'why' question sounds really judgemental and often makes the other person defensive, whereas a 'how' question opens up possibilities."

Quinn nods encouragingly. "Nice one. And what else?"

"I could really listen to the other person and give them 100% of my attention – rather than thinking about what I'm going to say next,"[7] Queenie replies. "Like the Stephen Covey quote: 'Most people do not listen with the intent to understand; they listen with the intent to reply.' That's so me – and if I'm really honest with you, sometimes I don't even wait for them to finish their sentence before I jump in."

Quinn nods again. "Mmm."

Queenie knows all this, yet somehow she forgets to do it. She is a little disappointed with herself but would never let on. With renewed determination, she takes a deep breath. "I could also use less judgemental and directive language. I often hear myself saying things like, 'Yeah, but you should / you ought to / the best way to do this is...' When I speak like this, people often nod politely at me and then, as if they haven't heard a word I've said, they do something completely different. Alternatively, sometimes they just get downright huffy."

---

7 For more information about Listening to Understand, go to www.LisaBrice.co.uk/bquickcoachingresources.

Quinn is sensitive to how Queenie often uses her brashness to hide how much she really cares. He is keen to encourage her to focus on what she wants rather than what she doesn't want. "That sounds good to me, and if you aren't using judgemental and directive language, what sort of language are you using?"

Thinking for a moment, Queenie answers, "Invitational language.[8] Saying things like 'and' instead of 'but'; 'You might choose to...'; 'How do you mean?'; 'Is there anything else?' Turning a statement into a question whenever possible."

"And is there anything else you could do?" Quinn probes.

Queenie looks up at the ceiling as she searches for inspiration. "I've heard you talk about Clean Language[9] and I think you described it as 'How do you ask a question without contaminating the other person's response?' It sounds like having an attitude of curiosity would be a great antidote to my normal judgemental stance. Have you got a book or a course you could recommend on Clean Language?"

Quinn responds, "Yes, for sure – there are a couple of great books and the woman I trained with was fantastic. I'll ping the information over later. And you have probably noticed me using questions like 'How do you mean?', 'In what way?', 'What would you like to have happen?', 'What does that get you?' and 'Is there anything else about ...?'"

Queenie has a flash of insight. "Oooh! I've just made the connection between the type of questions you use and some of the ones in the bQUICK® Coaching Model."

Quinn smiles to himself, secretly pleased that Queenie has recognised the Clean Questions implicit in the model. "My

---

8 For more information about Invitational Language, go to www.LisaBrice.co.uk/bquickcoachingresources.

9 For more information about Clean Language, go to www.LisaBrice.co.uk/bquickcoachingresources.

sense is that you have come up with some good ideas, Queenie. Which one are you most drawn to?"

Relaxing and feeling the tension ease out of her body, Queenie says, "I'm actually going to practise two ideas, as I think they go well together and will enable me to connect more fully with the other person. First, I'm going to ask more 'how' instead of 'why' questions. Second, I'm going to focus on what they're saying, rather than thinking about what I am going to say next, while reminding myself to listen with the intent to understand rather than to reply."

Quinn nods and smiles at Queenie. "Great – that makes sense and sounds like it will work really well for you. Do you want to buy me another coffee next week and you can tell me how brilliant you've been?"

"Yeah, same time next week, if that suits you? And of course I'm buying!" Queenie says cheekily.

Next week arrives and they snuggle into the same cosy chairs, with a large cappuccino and a chocolate chip muffin each.

Quinn gets right to it. "So, Queenie, how have you got on?"

Queenie loves to blow her own trumpet – although often it's a front to hide her insecurities. "As you would expect, Quinn, it's been brilliant! I had a review meeting with the project team we were talking about and it was like I was a different person. I prepared for the meeting and wrote out some 'how' questions that I thought might be useful."

Quinn grins at her. He knows her well. She can be quite sensitive and is keen to do things well.

Queenie continues. "I can see you're looking at me like you don't recognise me... it gets better! I started the meeting by running an appreciation exercise, which led everyone to feel really good about themselves and one another. I asked my 'how' questions and really listened to what everyone said. The ideas and solutions just seemed to flow, and I barely had to suggest anything – obviously, I couldn't resist adding my two pennies' worth every now and then.

"I feel my ability to ask good questions and really listen to understand is starting to develop. And I've completely smashed my belief that I've got all the best answers. As a team, we're beginning to collaborate well, partnering even, and coming up with innovative solutions together.

"I'm developing into a far more curious communicator. And, spookily, the team have gone up a gear – they're now pre-empting problems and coming to me with their own solutions. It's amazing! I can now get on with my own job rather than worrying about doing everyone else's."

Quinn is impressed. "Wow, what can I say? Well done."

Having relayed her success story, Queenie is delighted with herself and is even more determined to stay curious and not be as judgemental.

Quinn heads back to his office, pleased that he has helped Queenie improve her leadership skills. Her new style of questioning and listening has clearly enhanced her team's engagement, creativity and problem-solving abilities.

bQUICK® Wins:

Question the Situation, Stop Jumping to Conclusions and Be Less Judgemental

- Ask at least three open questions before giving your opinion; use 'how' questions in place of 'why' questions.

- Listen to understand, giving the other person all your attention.

- Use invitational language rather than directive language.

- Incorporate Clean Language questions to help facilitate the other person's thinking.

Chapter 3: Understand the Outcome

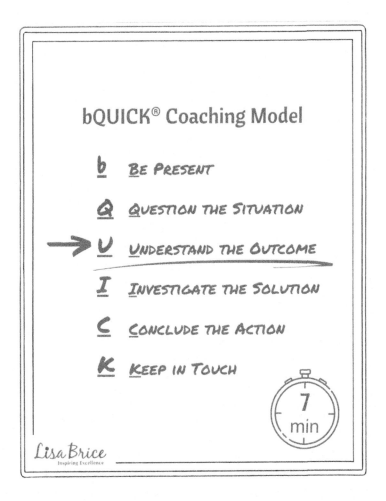

Udo is coming to the end of his monthly video call with his mentor, Uma. They have been working together for several months and now have a great relationship.

Drawing the session to a close, Uma asks, "So, Udo, is this a good enough place to leave it for today?"

Udo thinks for a moment. "Well, there is one more thing I'd

quite like your advice on, but I'm a little embarrassed to say."
Uma says encouragingly, "OK, we have about five minutes
left. You know this is a safe space. What would you like to
share?"
Udo flushes. "I've been given some feedback that I often
point out the negative in things. They said that I've a tendency
to talk about why something won't work, and I generally focus
on problems rather than solutions. And you know me, I do
love finding problems and I relish the challenge of analysing
them. I know I can be very risk averse at times, but I don't
think I'm that bad."
Uma senses the courage it is taking for Udo to share the
feedback he's received. "Oh, that sounds a bit tricky for you to
hear. I wonder if you might like to unpick it a bit?"
"Yeah, that would be good," Udo replies.
Uma smiles. "My sense is it might be more helpful for us to
have a coaching-style conversation rather than me give you
advice as your mentor. How about we re-contract for an extra
fifteen-minute coaching session now, if you've got time?"
Udo smiles back, feeling a sense of relief. "That would be
amazing, thank you.
Let's both pop for a quick comfort break and grab ourselves
a cup of tea."
Uma nods. "See you in five," she says, before she switches
off her camera.
While she boils the kettle, Uma does the HeartMath Quick
Coherence® Technique. She wants to ensure she is in an
optimum performance state for her coaching conversation
with Udo.
Back at her desk, Uma turns on her video again. "So, Udo,
tell me a bit more about what's going on for you."
Udo begins to open up. "The team were having a review of
our individual and collective strengths where we all received
feedback. The more I think about mine, the worse it seems to

get. I can't remember a single strength that was mentioned, and I'm only focusing on my weaknesses. I'm obsessing so much about the critical bits. It's like I've deleted any of the positive feedback about me or how I contribute to the team. And I suppose I'm starting to see that my response to the feedback is in itself negative."

Uma notices his body language is quite closed and she feels a sadness emanating from him. "That makes total sense to me. I get what you are saying." Even though they are on a video call, she trusts that Udo can pick up her genuine desire to support him. "So, what could your behaviour of focusing on the problem be trying to do for you?"

Udo looks confused. "Sorry, what do you mean exactly?"

"Whenever we have a behaviour or way of being, remember there will be an unconscious positive intention.[10] Your focusing on the negative will be attempting to do something useful for you," Uma elaborates.

Udo pauses to consider the question again. "Ah, I hadn't really thought of it like that. I was just framing it all as negative. I guess the positive intent might be to stop me or the team getting things wrong. Previously, when I have foreseen problems, it's stopped the company making some really costly mistakes. I'm now starting to see that spotting problems helps make me a good analyst, and pre-empting them is one of the reasons I'm great at scenario planning. And being a cautious person helps balance those members of the team who are more gung-ho."

Uma asks, "So, from what you are saying, I can see there are some key benefits to you having a problem-thinking[11]

---

10 For more information about Unconscious Positive Intentions, go to www.LisaBrice.co.uk/bquickcoachingresources.

11 For more information about Problem Thinking, go to www.LisaBrice.co.uk/bquickcoachingresources.

orientation. And I'm wondering if you want more behavioural flexibility?"

Udo sits up a bit straighter. "Yes."

"OK, great. In that case, would you value being able to offer solutions to the problems that you spot and develop more of an outcome-thinking[12] orientation?"

Udo nods and smiles.

Uma throws in her 'miracle question'[13] and asks, hypnotically: "If this coaching session is miraculously successful ... and you wake up tomorrow morning ... and this problem is completely solved ... how would you know this miracle has occurred?"

Udo scratches his head as he considers the question. "Well, I wouldn't get caught in a negative spiral of doubt and confusion. In a nutshell, my automatic default would be less problem-orientated."

Uma is keen to ensure Udo focuses on what he wants rather than what he doesn't want, so she asks, "And when you're less problem-orientated, then what happens?"

"I would be more solution-focused," Udo responds. "I'd have a better balance between seeing the problems and generating ideas to help the team."

Uma continues to keep Udo's attention on the outcome he wants. "And when you are more solution-focused, what does that get you?"

"I feel much more excited about all the different possibilities of us achieving our goals," Udo replies, with a big grin.

Uma probes further. "And is it within your control to generate ideas to help the team achieve their goals?"

---

[12] For more information about Outcome Thinking, go to www.LisaBrice.co.uk/bquickcoachingresources.

[13] For more information about The Miracle Question, go to www.LisaBrice.co.uk/bquickcoachingresources.

"Yes, I guess it is. But it isn't my natural style." Udo's shoulders slump as he replies.

Uma pauses, makes firm eye contact with Udo, and smiles across the ether at him. "Udo, I'm just going to flag something to you, if that's OK?"

Udo nods.

"What is the focus of the statement you've just made, 'but it isn't my natural style' – is that problem- or outcome-orientated?"

The penny drops. "Oops! I just told you about the problem again, didn't I?"

Uma is determined to keep Udo's attention on the outcome. "Yeah, so what would you like to have happen?"

Udo takes a deep breath as he considers what he really wants. "I'd like to have sufficient self-awareness that I can differentiate between problems – 'away from' thinking – and solutions – 'towards' thinking – giving me a choice of where I channel my attention."

Now it is Uma's turn to grin. "That sounds like an outcome to me! What could you do to move closer to your goal?"

Udo responds, "I could remember this feeling of excitement that focusing on my goals can give me. From our conversation today, I now realise there is a big difference between moving 'away from' the pain of something and moving 'towards' the gain of something."

Wanting to reinforce his insights, Uma says, "Yes, an 'away from' triggers momentum and yet, to sustain motivation, we need a compelling goal.

How will you remember this in the future?"

Udo replies, "You can't hit a target you can't see, and if we are only concerned about the problems, we take our eye off where we want to get to. Ooh, look at me, I've done it again, haven't I?" He's on a roll. "I'll rephrase that – keep your eyes on the prize, Udo!"

bQUICK® COACHING

Uma nods encouragingly in acknowledgement of his improving self-awareness. "So, what else would give you a choice of where you put your attention?"

Udo becomes more and more animated as his confidence grows. "It would be great to have more choice and awareness about the words I use. During the team review I was told that I use the word 'don't' a lot. They highlighted that apparently our brains don't initially hear the word 'don't'. As an example, they said, 'Don't think of a purple spotted elephant.' Of course, I immediately thought of a purple spotted elephant before realising they had said 'Don't think of...' I think they described this phenomena as an embedded command."[14]

Uma is keen to expand his understanding. "What real-life examples of using the word 'don't' can you think of and how could they be heard?"

Udo pauses to think for a moment. "'Don't worry' could be heard as 'worry'; 'don't hesitate to call me' as 'hesitate to call me'; 'don't take too long to think about it' as 'take too long to think about it'."

Uma asks, "If 'don't' is the problem, what is the solution?"

"I could experiment with using other words instead of 'don't'. For example, instead of 'don't worry', I could say 'stay calm'; instead of 'don't hesitate to call me', 'please call me'."

Delighted, Uma recaps with a wink. "Yes. So, you've got don't use 'don't' as an embedded command. Instead of telling people what you don't want, you can tell them what you do want. And you now have your eyes firmly focused on the prize. And what else could you do?"

Udo says, "I could find even more motivation for myself to move 'away from' the pain and 'towards' the gain."

Uma enquires, "And what might give you more motivation?"

---

14 For more information about Embedded Commands, go to www.LisaBrice.co.uk/bquickcoachingresources.

44

"Perhaps if I can make the goal more exciting somehow?" Udo ponders.

"And how might you do that?" Uma probes further.

Udo considers this. "Maybe the first part of making the goal more exciting is to make the problem worse? Yeah... that might work. I could imagine the consequence of a worst-case scenario and then exaggerate it to make it even worse. And then I could also imagine amplifying the effect of a possible solution on the desired outcome to make it even better."

"Sounds like you are on a roll. And is there anything else?" Uma encourages.

"I could not only think about the impact for me personally, but also the consequences for the team and the company. Imagining how everyone else could benefit will give me even more motivation. This will make the goal even more enticing for me!" Udo triumphantly exclaims as he starts to wriggle in his chair.

Uma paraphrases, "So, what I'm hearing you say is that exaggerating the consequences of the problem and exaggerating the implications of the solution gives you way more motivation."

"Yeah, for sure!" Udo glows.

Uma feels herself getting caught up in Udo's excitement. "All your ideas around creating more choice sound great! Which ones are you most enthusiastic to try?"

Udo pauses, sits up straight, breathes deeply and smiles at Uma. "I'm going to find compelling goals and remind myself to keep my eyes on the prize."

Uma nods approvingly. "Great – that sounds like it has energy for you. Do you want to let me know how you get on at our next mentoring session, or would you like to touch base sooner?"

"Next month is fine," Udo replies.

In bringing their time together to a close, Uma says,

"Perfect. Before we finish, I want to put my mentoring hat back on and see if you have heard of the PRO Model?"

"No, I haven't. Tell me more," says Udo.

"The PRO Model[15] is a series of questions created by James Lawley & Penny Tompkins *(Coach the Coach,* Feb 2006*)*. They were inspired by David Grove's Clean Language work. PRO stands for Problem, Remedy, Outcome. 'Problem' is what you don't want, 'Remedy' sounds like what you want, but is still moving away from the problem rather than towards the solution, and 'Outcome' is the goal you want. I think of it a bit like a set of traffic lights – 'Problem' is red and you can't go anywhere, 'Remedy' is amber and you are getting ready to go, 'Outcome' is green and you are free to go," Uma explains.

Udo looks intrigued. "Thanks, Uma, that sounds really interesting. I'll do some research and see how it fits with me."

Uma asks, "Is this an OK place to leave it today?"

Nodding, Udo smiles. "Yes – I'm good, thanks."

Next month comes around quickly. Udo and Uma are reconnecting. Uma enquires, "Before we start your mentoring session, I'd love to hear how you got on after our coaching conversation?"

"Well Uma, I've been doing OK. Actually, I've been doing really well. And the fact that I didn't say 'not too bad' tells me how much progress I'm making. And, in the interests of keeping my eyes on the prize, I want to tell you about a positive experience I had. A member of my team came to me with a problem and wanted some advice. I suggested that we explore what solutions might be available to her by using the bQUICK® Coaching Model instead.

"I kept my focus on her, and I was really pleased that I was able to stay present. And, by holding my attention on her and

---

15 For more information about The PRO Model, go to www.LisaBrice.co.uk/bquickcoachingresources.

listening with curiosity, I noticed the connection between us deepened.

"The PRO Model questions you suggested worked well, particularly the outcome question, 'So what would you like to have happen?' As a result, the solutions she came up with turned out brilliantly.

"I've proven to myself that I've got the skills to be solution-focused as well as to problem-solve – I now know I can do this and I'm noticing I'm naturally becoming increasingly outcome-orientated! I've got much more choice about whether I focus on the problem and what I don't want, or focus on the prize and what I do want."

Uma is delighted for Udo. "Wow. I'm impressed."

"Thanks so much, Uma. I really can't tell you how helpful your coaching was. Actually, delete that – I can tell you. Your mini-coaching session was genuinely life-changing," Udo says, grinning.

Udo is really pleased with the progress he has made in only a month. He's now confident in his ability to spot the difference between problem thinking and outcome thinking. And he's surprised how he is automatically leaning towards finding compelling goals and coming up with solutions.

Uma is left pondering the difference between coaching and mentoring, and how they are both valuable in different situations: coaching, where she asks questions to empower others and encourages them to do the bulk of the thinking and talking, and mentoring, where she offers her expertise, information, advice, and sometimes even a bit of hand-holding. It confirms to her that whilst a coaching style can have a place in mentoring, or indeed any leadership conversation, unsolicited advice-giving and mentoring definitely doesn't have a place in coaching.

bQUICK® Wins:

Understand the Outcome
and Move On from the Problem

- Focus the other person's thinking on what they want (the outcome) rather than what they don't want (the problem).

- Find alternatives to the embedded commands you might typically use.

- Exaggerate the consequences of both the problem and the outcome to increase motivation.

- Use the PRO Model and its traffic light system to ensure you have identified a goal.

Chapter 4: Investigate the Solution

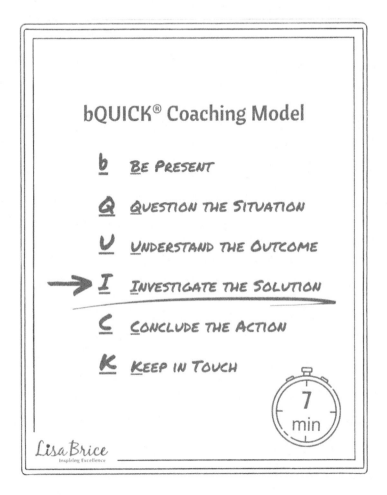

bQUICK® Coaching Model

b BE PRESENT

Q QUESTION THE SITUATION

U UNDERSTAND THE OUTCOME

I INVESTIGATE THE SOLUTION

C CONCLUDE THE ACTION

K KEEP IN TOUCH

7 min

Lisa Brice
Inspiring Excellence

Imogen has set up an informal on-boarding meeting with Ida, her new team member. They are enjoying getting to know each other in a quaint little coffee shop down the road from the office.

Imogen enthuses, "I'm so glad Kao recommended I recruit you. I can see why he was so impressed with you when you two met on your four-day coaching training."

Ida grins. "Yeah, me too. I really enjoyed meeting him and I loved the training we did together."

"I remember Kao glowing about the session working with horses.[16] That sounds wonderful – and right up my street!" Imogen smiles as she takes a sip of coffee. "How did you find it?"

Ida's face lights up. "Oh my gosh, yeah, it's right up my street too! It was such an amazing and unique experience. And it was a bonus I wasn't expecting to find on a coaching training."

"What was so amazing about the experience?" Imogen asks, enjoying the buzz.

"It was awesome to feel what a powerful connection you can create without any words. I managed to build incredible rapport with the horse just by being present and using my body language. The horse chose to follow me without a leading rope or anything. It was incredible," Ida says, beaming.

"That does sound awesome! What else did you learn?"

Ida pauses to consider. "By being present, I learnt to tap into the wisdom of my body. As a result, I got to experience embodied leadership in a way I never had before. The connection with the horse was magical and deeply profound. I'm sure it will stay with me forever."

"Wow, I'd love to have a go myself," exclaims Imogen. Enjoying their chemistry, she decides now is a good time to steer the conversation towards how they can work together productively. "I'm so excited you have joined us, not just because of the unique skills you bring but also because we will now have someone who can offer in-house coaching within our team."

Ida settles back into her chair; she is feeling really

---

16 For more information about coaching with horses and Horses for Courses®, go to www.LisaBrice.co.uk/bquickcoachingresources.

comfortable with her new manager. "I'm really looking forward to having more coaching responsibilities. Coaching was one of the things I loved most about my previous job."

Imogen smiles at Ida. She can sense the rapport growing between them. "As I'm starting to see the impact coaching can have, it is becoming a real passion of mine too. And I'm impressed at what a great way it is to develop people and unlock their potential."

"I'm delighted to hear we share a love of coaching and a keen interest in developing our teams," enthuses Ida.

Imogen beams back. "Yes, although unlike you, I'm at the beginning of my journey and I've not done much coaching myself yet. I'm really keen to learn more, although in truth I'm still a little bit nervous about starting to practise."

"Thank you for being so open with me," Ida says. "I remember how I felt when I was at the beginning of my coaching journey. It takes a bit of a leap of faith to start feeling comfortable."

Imogen smiles awkwardly. "Well, I guess I'm going to need to take that leap of faith pretty soon. As managers, we've all agreed to adopt a coaching style to our conversations."

Ida nods. "Yes, I was excited when Kao told me the company was going to implement a coaching culture by introducing everyone to the bQUICK® Coaching Model. I think it is a fantastic idea to trial using it. From my experience, it is an amazingly simple structure to follow and a brilliant tool. I love using it – and I'm a qualified coach. But I've seen it used perfectly competently by complete beginners. In fact, it's that simple, I imagine anyone could use it."

"Yeah, I'm really looking forward to being proficient in using the model," Imogen replies. "Are you happy if we move on and start to explore how we can best work together?"

"If it's anything like this meeting, I'm sure we will be fine," Ida says, trying to keep things light.

Imogen says, "Yes, I'm really enjoying getting to know you and I'm assuming we will work well together. And you know what they say about assuming! So, I'm curious to find out how you like and don't like to be managed."

Ida feels a little bit of pressure and, because of the trust they have developed, decides to answer honestly. "For me, it's really important to have open dialogue and for my boss to give me specific feedback about what works well and what doesn't work so well for them."

Imogen raises her eyebrows and nods. "Thank you for saying that, because it dawns on me that I'm very comfortable encouraging people. And if I'm honest, I'm a bit shy about telling people what doesn't work for me. Now you've mentioned it, I'm happy to try and incorporate it in my feedback to you."

"And how might you incorporate it? Oops, sorry... that's inappropriate. I've gone into coaching mode!" utters Ida with a nervous little laugh.

Imogen laughs too. "Nice catch. I'm curious you went straight into questioning mode; I don't know if I would have."

Ida grins. "Yeah, I've just realised when I hear the word 'try', I have a knee jerk reaction to coach. Having a coaching style is pretty ingrained in me. If I were a stick of rock and you cut me in half, you would read 'coaching' all the way through."

Curious, Imogen asks, "So, if you stay with your reflex to coach, what question would you ask me next?"

Ida replies, "If you don't go into questioning mode, what mode would you go into?"

Imogen says, "I don't know."

Ida smiles gently. "And if you did know, what might you say?"

After a short pause, Imogen says, "I'd guess that I usually just tell people what to do."

"So, if your tendency is to go into tell mode, how does that serve you?" Ida asks.

Imogen scratches her head and, after some thought, says, "Hmm, that's a great question. You've really got me thinking..."

"I realise I'm asking coaching questions again. Is that OK with you?" Ida checks. "Because it's not sitting quite right with me."

Imogen is keen to reassure Ida. "Yeah, another nice catch. Of course it feels a bit odd, especially with me being your new boss. It's really important to us, as a company, that we challenge the normal hierarchies. We appreciate part of developing a true coaching culture is knowing that anyone can coach anyone."

Impressed, Ida says, "Wow, that shows me the company really does walk the talk. With your permission, I've had an idea. How about we continue with me in questioning mode and I'll start following the bQUICK® Coaching Model? That way you get to experience the benefits of being a bQUICK® coachee. And, if you like, I can walk you through the structure at the same time."

"Yes, great idea! That sounds like a good plan and really helpful." Imogen beams.

Feeling reassured, Ida dives in. "OK, I'll keep my coaching hat on, and every now and then take it off to explain the stages. bQUICK® is a mnemonic, so you'll find it easy to remember the six steps. First is **'b' – Be Present.**"

Ida takes a moment. "You may have noticed me pause to take a deep breath, clear my head, and centre myself. This is often all I need to do to get present and connect with the person I'm coaching. Sometimes I may also choose to match and mirror the other person to build a bit more rapport."

Imogen nods. "Thanks, that all makes sense."

Ida continues. "Now we get to my favourite few steps, where we enter the exploration phase, remembering to stay curious. Second is **'Q' – Question the Situation.** You mentioned earlier you often tell people what to do. Is that still what you want to explore?"

Imogen takes a sip of coffee. "Yes, I think so."

"Perfect. Say a bit more about where you are now with regards to telling people what to do."

"For me, sometimes it works really well, and sometimes it feels like I'm being bossy or becoming the Advice Monster,"[17] replies Imogen.

Ida, raising an eyebrow curiously, says, "Tell me a bit more about the Advice Monster."

"At a recent training, we were introduced to the Advice Monster and the Drama Triangle. Since then, I've noticed how often I can fall into both of these traps," responds Imogen.

Ida leans forward in her chair. "I already know about the Drama Triangle, but I've not heard of the Advice Monster. Can you tell me a little bit more?"

Imogen nods. "If I remember correctly, the Advice Monster comes out when we give unsolicited advice. And I think we get a dopamine hit from it, which is why we feel good when we do it.

"We were shown that this can overlap with the Rescuer position in the Drama Triangle[18] in that we can receive a similar dopamine hit when we jump in and rescue people by giving them advice. And we were told how much more empowering and effective it can be for people when they are trusted and allowed to come up with their own ideas and solutions."

"Ooh, thanks," Ida says. "I can see how 'advice monstering' can overlap with rescuing. I have my own understanding of

---

17 For more information about the Advice Monster, go to www.LisaBrice.co.uk/bquickcoachingresources.
18 For more information about the Drama Triangle, go to www.LisaBrice.co.uk/bquickcoachingresources.

what 'rescuing' means in the Drama Triangle and I'm wondering what 'rescuing' means to you?"

Imogen slowly exhales. "From my perspective, rescuing comes from a genuine desire to help people. However, this well-intentioned approach can inadvertently manifest as persecution, since it can imply a lack of faith in the other person's abilities and competencies. This is why Persecutor and Rescuer are both drawn next to each other, at the top of the triangle, with Victim down at the bottom."

"That's in line with my understanding of the Triangle too," Ida acknowledges. "Now we know we are on the same page, how does getting into tell mode play out for you?"

Thinking to herself, Imogen takes a deep breath. "I tend to jump in and give people advice on what they should do, instead of encouraging them to come up with their own solutions. I see this as rescuing them, by giving them my opinion of what to do, instead of giving them time to come up with their own ideas. I guess it can make it easy for them to perceive me as attacking them rather than helping them. In Drama Triangle language, they see me as a Persecutor rather than a Rescuer, and either way I've put them in the place of Victim."

"Mmm, that all makes sense to me. Is there anything else?" Ida probes.

Imogen replies, "Yes. Once I've put someone in the Victim position they are likely to defend themselves and get drawn into the Persecutor or Rescuer position. When they are in either place, I then get pulled into the Victim position myself – and then the Drama Triangle phenomenon will be in effect, and the drama will no doubt escalate."

"What else would be useful for me to know about this?" questions Ida.

"When I rescue someone and put them in the place of Victim by giving them my solutions, it's unsolicited advice.

Neuroscience shows that when people receive advice they haven't asked for, they get a flood of cortisol similar to the amount of cortisol they receive when they are under stress or being attacked. And that is the last thing I want... I'm only trying to help!"

Ida nods and leans back in her chair. "Wow, my head is in a bit of a spin as I listen to you explain it! How are you doing?"

"Yeah, I feel like I've been in a bit of a whirlwind!" Imogen smiles.

They both laugh. Ida says, "So, you've told me about how in the past you jumped in and gave people advice. If I pause for a moment to walk you through the bQUICK® model, I could easily assume you've now got enough information to 'Q – Question the Situation', but I'd always make sure by asking if there is anything else. Is there anything else?"

"Thanks. Now you mention it, I tend to feel the need to rescue more when either the team or I are under time pressure," Imogen says.

Ida smiles encouragingly. "And just to double check I have all the relevant information about the situation, is there anything else?"

"Nope, I think that's about it," Imogen replies, shaking her head.

Ida continues. "In that case we can move on. Third is **U – Understand the Outcome.** So, now we understand the situation and where the person is at with it, this next step is about finding out and making sure we know where they want to get to. It is important to remember to clarify their goal, as focusing on an outcome is an integral part of every coaching conversation. With that in mind, and given that you don't want to rescue, even when you are under time pressure, what would you like to have happen?"

Imogen ponders this. "Well, I get annoyed when people jump in and try to rescue me, so I can see why people might get annoyed or resent it when I do the same."

Ida smiles, and asks, "So, if you find jumping in and rescuing annoying, what would you like to have happen instead?"

"I want to be supportive of the creative process and be comfortable allowing the other person to come up with their own solutions."

"And when you allow the other person to come up with their own solutions, then what happens?" Ida probes.

Imogen is impressed at Ida's skill in clarifying what she wants. "I get to show my team that I trust them."

Ida is starting to relax and enjoy herself. "And when you do that, what does that get you?"

"I get to empower my team and cultivate a culture of personal responsibility, accountability and resourcefulness!" exclaims Imogen.

"And is this within your control?" queries Ida.

"Yes, absolutely," replies Imogen confidently.

Ida beams. "Great! Now we have a positive outcome we can move on to the fourth step: **I – Investigate the Solution.** Here you can continue to be curious and help them explore various options to enable them to achieve their desired outcome. What solutions have you tried so far?"

"I've tried not to tell people what to do and keep my ideas to myself. But then I find I just disguise my opinion in the form of asking questions to lead the person to the solution I've already thought of!" Imogen laughs nervously.

"I know that one. What have you tried that worked?" Ida asks, supportively.

"I sometimes find sitting on my hands helps stop me giving advice, even when I've got a brilliant idea. Although I'm not sure why sitting on my hands stops me speaking, it seems to work!" Imogen says.

Nodding, Ida continues to probe. "What else could you do?"

Imogen grins as possible solutions spring to mind. "I could

ensure that when someone comes to me with a problem, I send them away to come up with two solutions by themself. That way, I educate my people to come to me with a problem and a couple of possible solutions of their own. Then, between us, we can explore them and agree on the best course of action."

Ida nods and smiles.

Imogen continues. "And I suppose if their solutions are ridiculous, I can ask them a series of questions so they future pace[19] the likely consequences of how their ideas might play out."

"And what sort of questions could you ask to future pace their ideas?" Ida asks.

Imogen replies, "I suppose I could ask questions like, 'And then what might happen?', 'And if you did that, what might be the consequence?', 'What could be the impact of X on Y?', and so on."

Ida is keen to support Imogen's momentum so merely says, "Mmm."

"And I could do what I've noticed you are doing with me, Ida. I could use silence to encourage the person to think for themself. I'm realising giving people space is a really powerful way of asking a question non-verbally."

Ida is pleased with how the conversation is going and decides to be a little provocative. "These all sound like good ideas to me and I sense that you know exactly what to do. So, I'm curious – how come you aren't consistently allowing people to come up with their own solutions already?"

Imogen pauses and looks down. "Ooh, tough question. That's made me stop and think. I guess I just really care about people and want to 'rescue' them when they're struggling. It's

---

19 For more information about Future Pacing, go to www.LisaBrice.co.uk/bquickcoachingresources.

just an ingrained response for me to offer advice."

"So, when your response isn't ingrained anymore and you aren't offering advice, what would you have let go of?" Ida challenges.

Imogen slowly exhales as she thinks to herself, "Wow, I definitely made a good recruitment decision." Out loud, she says, "I'd have let go of my own ego and recognised that I don't have to have all the solutions. Someone might have a great idea I haven't thought of."

Ida and Imogen smile at each other. They both sense that something profound has been said.

"I think we are ready to move on to the fifth step: **C – Conclude the Action**," Ida suggests. Leaning forward and making firm eye contact, she continues, "So having come up with some great ideas, what are you committing to do, moving forward?"

Imogen takes a moment to reflect before responding, "I'm going to trust my team more and use the bQUICK® Coaching Model to encourage them to get creative and come up with their own solutions."

Ida has a warm glow of connection in her tummy. "Well, I'm really excited to be working with you, Imogen."

Impressed with Ida's coaching style, Imogen says, "Me too, Ida. I'm delighted to have you on our team. I think we can do some great things together. Let's keep in touch and check in on how our respective styles are working for each other. Please feel free to give me any feedback, and I'll do the same for you. And I'll remember to tell you what doesn't work for me, as well as all the things you are doing brilliantly well."

"Thanks! And you beat me to the final step: **K – Keep in Touch**," Ida says. She feels relieved that their conversation has gone so well. "I feel like I'm starting to understand what you want from me and your team members. As well as getting to know you better, I really appreciate us having this welcome chat."

A couple of weeks pass, and Ida is integrating really well into the team. She and Imogen are back in the coffee shop having a quick catch up and progress update.

Imogen is delighted with Ida. "I'm really pleased with how well you are settling in. I can already see such a difference in your team. I want to check in with you about my leadership style and make sure it's working for you."

"Thank you. I'm really enjoying being here and it's a fantastic team to be part of. And I'm particularly grateful for the specific feedback you have given me about what's working and not working for you," Ida says. "I'm loving the way we bounce ideas around between us. I've noticed you giving me the space to come up with potential solutions to any problems we have encountered, and I really appreciate it. It's boosted my confidence in my own abilities and made me feel welcome at the same time."

Imogen leans forward to show she is engaged. "Thank you. I've enjoyed exploring options with you. Through our debates, I've developed a real trust in your judgement; I've also been impressed with your creativity. And I've got some feedback for you from our coaching conversation a couple of weeks ago. I have been flexing my style with other members of the team and I'm seeing some great results. I've also got a much better handle on the bQUICK® Coaching Model."

They finish their coffees and head back to the office.

Having got some great results from experimenting with her new style, Imogen feels motivated to continue to encourage people to investigate their own solutions, rather than jumping in to give her own opinion or advice.

From their initial meeting, Ida was particularly pleased with herself as she was courageous enough to ask some challenging and thought-provoking questions. She understands that coaching certainly isn't the soft option. It takes real courage to ask insightful and powerful questions, particularly of her boss.

 bQUICK® Wins:

Investigate Solutions and Don't Offer Advice

- *Avoid `rescuing'. Instead, encourage people to come to you with a brief overview of the situation and at least two ideas about how to resolve it.*

- *Ask a series of questions to enable the other person to future pace their solutions, checking the possible consequences and how realistic they are.*

- *Practise using silence to give the other person space to think.*

- *Trust others will come up with solutions you might not think of; a benefit of teamwork is that the whole is greater than the sum of its parts.*

Chapter 5: Conclude the Action

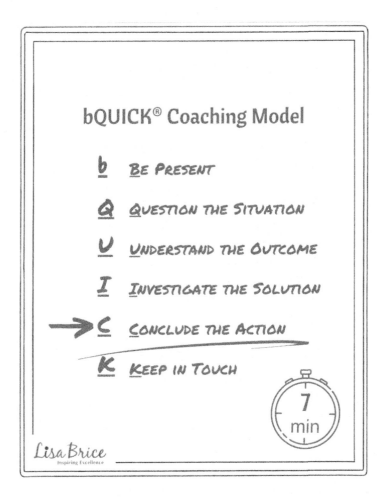

bQUICK® Coaching Model

b BE PRESENT

Q QUESTION THE SITUATION

U UNDERSTAND THE OUTCOME

I INVESTIGATE THE SOLUTION

→ **C** CONCLUDE THE ACTION

K KEEP IN TOUCH

7 min

Lisa Brice
Inspiring Excellence

Christina is on a party planning video call with her cousin Cam and other members of their family. It's Christina's parents' 50th wedding anniversary soon, which is going to be held on their home island of Kefalonia. People will be travelling from all corners of the world to celebrate together.

Cam is congratulating Christina on all her hard work

arranging everything. "I think you've nailed it, Cuz."

Christina's uncle chimes in. "Yeah, I reckon you could become a professional party planner."

"Thanks guys, that means a lot!" Christina says. Then she sighs.

Cam is concerned that Christina isn't her usual cheerful self, so he sends her a private message in the chat. *How are you doing? You don't seem your normal self.*

Christina replies, *Yeah! Pulling everything together has been exhausting. And I've got work stuff going on too.*

Cam types back, *I wish we weren't on opposite sides of the world – I'd give you a hug.*

A virtual hug from Australia is perfect, Christina responds, adding a smiley emoji.

Do you want a chat after this call? Cam offers.

Christina answers, *Ooh, yes please, but I need to clear my head first and go for a run.*

Cam signs off, *Give me a ring when you are back. XX*

After her shower, Christina video-calls Cam. "Thanks for reaching out and making the time to chat. I've really appreciated having you as a sounding board in the past."

Cam responds, "No worries. I'm all yours – well, for the next ten minutes at least. What's up?"

"Planning a party abroad has been quite a thing, especially with so many moving parts. And to tell you the truth, arranging the party has been quite fun; it's the work stuff that is really bothering me," Christina explains.

"Ah, I wondered what was going on when you sighed earlier. Do you want to talk about the work stuff?" Cam asks, tilting his head.

"Yeah. I was feeling too stressed earlier to have a useful conversation. Now I've been for a run, it would be really helpful to talk it through with you and hopefully then I can enjoy the weekend." Christina smiles.

"OK, go for it." Cam smiles back encouragingly.

"Generally, things have been pretty good at work recently, and we've been on target with most of our projects. But I've got this one guy, Tom, who just doesn't seem to be pulling his weight." Christina rolls her eyes. "He's agreeing to things and then doesn't deliver. He always seems to have an excuse as to why something hasn't happened or how something is someone else's fault. As I talk about it, I can feel myself getting frustrated again."

Sensing Christina's annoyance, Cam responds with empathy. "Of course. I can sense your irritation emanating all the way from little old England! I'd be frustrated too. And what else would be good for me to know?"

"Well, as I've told you before, I'm a pretty laissez-faire sort of manager. I'm not someone who needs to know all the details; I'm more a big picture person. I tend to trust my people to get on with things and only come to me if there's a problem. However, with Tom I don't trust him; I feel like he's a slippery fish and I can't nail him down."

Cam wants to make sure that this is the full extent of the problem. "And is there anything else about all this?"

Christina shrugs her shoulders and sighs. "Nope, I think that's about it."

Happy to move on, Cam asks, "And what would you like to have happen?"

Christina takes a moment to consider what outcome she wants. "Well, I'd like to be able to hold Tom accountable for his performance and to be able to get him to agree to something and stick to it."

"And when you hold Tom to account, what does that get you?" Cam probes.

"More confidence that the job is going to get done in a timely manner," Christina says.

"And is it within your control to hold Tom accountable for

his performance?" Cam asks.

Feeling slightly conflicted, Christina replies, "Yes, I guess it is. And it just isn't my typical leadership style."

Cam wants to clarify if that's what Christina really wants. "I've just heard you say you want to know that 'the job is going to get done in a timely manner'."

Christina sighs to herself again. Cam is really holding her to account. Reluctantly, and perhaps a little petulantly, she replies, "Oh OK, I guess I'll just have to flex and adapt my style then."

Cam smiles. "Nice one. So, how could you flex and adapt your style with Tom?"

"I'm not sure," Christina murmurs, feeling like she has hit a stumbling block.

Knowing that deep down everyone has more ideas than they are initially aware of, Cam challenges, "And if you were sure, what would you say?"

Christina takes a moment and reconsiders the question. "Well, our relationship could do with a bit of work. I've not had much one-to-one time with him recently."

"Mmm, what else?" Cam asks.

Begrudgingly, Christina goes on. "I guess I could try and improve our connection and my level of rapport with him?"

Cam nods. "Well, you and I both know you can't do much without good rapport! And ...?" He deliberately lets his question tail off.

Christina takes up the mantle. "Often, I just tell him to get on with it. Instead, I could ask more questions about what he's intending to do, and then I could nail him down to a detailed plan. And, heaven forbid, I could even get him to commit to an agreed timescale."

Cam has been matching Christina's body language and notices that she is starting to relax. He smiles encouragingly at her.

Christina continues, "I guess he's pretty 'big chunk'[20] in his thinking, like me. I suppose it might help both of us to get into the nitty-gritty of the detail. And we could get specific about what his 'implementation intentions'[21] are – the who, the what, the when, the where, the how."

Cam nods. "I like the sound of that one. And is there anything else?"

"I think it's about digging a bit deeper and checking his level of commitment to whatever we're talking about. Sometimes I suspect he's just nodding and telling me what he thinks I want to hear so I'll just go away."

Cam wants to keep Christina talking, so he merely says, "Hmm."

Christina's mind flashes back to her early career. "And I could borrow the question my old boss often asked me: 'What has got your DNA all over it?' He said this when he wanted to challenge me to take responsibility for something."

Satisfied Christina has come up with some workable solutions, Cam asks, "Well, they all seem like pretty sensible approaches. What are you going to go with?"

Christina pauses to contemplate her options. "I'm going to set up a one-to-one meeting with Tom. I'm keen to build our rapport. And I'll ask him to run through his three most pressing projects and get specific about the details. I'll also check his level of motivation and commitment to achieving the deadlines."

Cam nods and asks, "When are you going to have your meeting?"

Christina gives a wry smile. "Nice one – I see what you're

---

[20] For more information about Big and Small Chunk Thinking, go to www.LisaBrice.co.uk/bquickcoachingresources.

[21] For more information about Implementation Intentions, go to www.LisaBrice.co.uk/bquickcoachingresources.

doing there, Cuz! I'll arrange it after our next ops meeting, which is the week before the party."

"Great! You can tell me all about it then, over a glass of Ouzo," says Cam, grinning.

Christina pretends to gag. "You know I hate that stuff! Thanks so much, you're a star."

In no time at all, everyone is in Kefalonia. The party is in full swing. Just before the dancing starts, Cam and Christina find a quiet corner for a quick catch up.

Cam says, "Fab party. Well done, you! Before the mayhem kicks off, I'm keen to hear how you got on with Tom."

Christina puts her hand on Cam's arm. "It all went really well, especially thanks to your coaching."

Feeling really pleased, Cam says, "I just listened; you did all the thinking and talking!"

Christina smiles, and winks at Cam. "Well, that's what makes you a great coach! And the upshot was the meeting with Tom was a real success. I didn't want us to be disturbed so we stayed in the boardroom after our ops meeting. Initially, I focused on building the rapport between us, by reflecting his energy, body language, the pace and tonality of his voice.

"As I matched and mirrored him, a real sense of calm came over me. I discovered he's even more laid back than I thought he was. And I got the sense he doesn't like to be rushed and is often quite deliberate in what he does.

"I asked for lots of information about his projects and their deadlines. I was super proud of a profound question I asked: 'On a scale of one to ten, how committed are you?' It revealed Tom could only give his commitment a score of four for one of his projects.

"Between us, we then flushed out the reason was he didn't believe we had the right 'implementation intentions' to complete that project on time. We kicked around some ideas and made some important amendments, so he had confidence in the whos, the whats, the whens, the wheres and the hows. This gave him the confidence to change his score from a four to an eight!

"It's so nice to realise that I absolutely can have the flexibility and capability to get into the finer details of things. And so does Tom, actually.

"I now believe in the importance of getting specific and asking lots of questions about what people are committing to, and how they are going to do it. When I hold someone to account, I'm in fact supporting them in achieving their outcomes, rather than interfering.

"That's a big shift for me. It's proved to me that digging into the detail actually helps facilitate other people's thinking. When people are empowered to think for themselves, they feel more motivated and everyone wins. And this leads to business success!"

Cam is delighted for Christina. "Well, I'd say that calls for a drink!" They head for the bar.

Christina is happy with how she handled the meeting with Tom and is keen to continue getting into the detail more often and practising holding people to account. She's now confident this will increase responsibility, accountability and ownership in her team.

Cam is pleased that, by being a sounding board, he was able to support his cousin in flexing her leadership style. He is really impressed it enabled her to make such remarkable progress with a challenging team member.

bQUICK® wins:

Conclude the Action and Stop Letting People Off the Hook

- Pay attention to the relationship. Ensure you build rapport and maintain your connection.

- Check the levels of motivation and commitment.

- Ask specifically what's going to be done and when it will be done by.

- Get details about the `implementation intentions'
        — how the task will be achieved.

Chapter 6: Keep in Touch

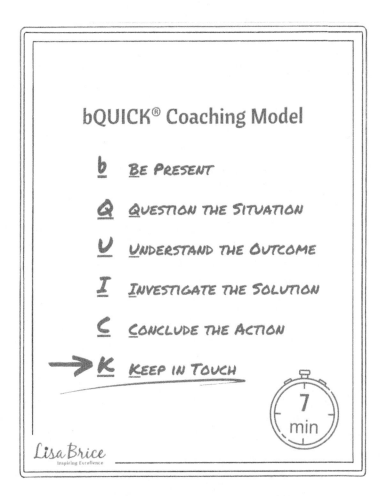

Kao is at an annual NLP conference. Walking down the corridor, deep in thought, he literally bumps into somebody. "Oh, I'm so sorry!"

Karl says with a smile of recognition, "So you should be, my old friend – I see you're day dreaming again! I was hoping to see you here."

Kao looks down, struggling to make eye contact. He's embarrassed, as he remembers he promised to get back to Karl with some information after the last time they met up. "I'm so sorry I didn't send over your friend Joe's NLP Master Practitioner modelling project – I completely forgot, and then as time passed I felt awkward and didn't know how to handle it."

Karl shrugs his shoulders. "No worries. I'd forgotten you said you would send it. And I've missed not hearing from you."

Kao is keen to make amends. "I'm sorry, I should've got back to you. Have you got time for a quick catch-up now?"

Not one to bear grudges, Karl grins. "Love to. And to be honest, I'm not brilliant at keeping in touch either."

Grabbing cups of tea, they find a quiet corner where they can stand at a tall table and chat. After the initial pleasantries, the conversation turns to how they are getting on at their respective companies.

Karl opens up. "Some of the relationships with my colleagues are deteriorating. And it is particularly bad with one woman, Rebecca. Have you got time to listen to this?"

Kao smiles at his friend. "Sure – my next session isn't for another ten minutes."

Karl gives Kao a look of gratitude. "Thanks. It would be great to talk to someone outside the business who doesn't know the personalities. I'm sure you will be able to give me an unbiased perspective. I'm worried that my relationship with Rebecca is soon going to break down completely. She just doesn't seem to trust me anymore. Things aren't brilliant with my other colleagues either. I used to think I was good at my job."

Kao nods to acknowledge he understands. "OK, I can tell that you are upset, and seem anxious and concerned about what is happening."

Karl lowers his gaze and murmurs, "Yeah."

Kao smiles and takes a couple of deep breaths. It's easy for him to manage his emotional state, as he isn't hooked into the company dynamic. Wanting to see if Karl has too much 'charge' around the situation for a helpful discussion, he checks, "Are you ready to talk about this now, or would another time be better for you?"

Karl leans back and rolls his shoulders. "Actually, now would be great because I'm a little less charged than when I'm at work. I get really uptight and annoyed about it there. And I'd really value your opinion."

"Great. What's going on then?" Kao asks.

Karl splurges, "Well, I'm crazy busy at work and am being pulled in a million different directions. We're in the middle of a huge change programme and have been for the last six months. I don't seem to have the time to consistently follow up with people. I've three different reporting lines, so I'm constantly juggling loads of priorities. Rebecca often has to chase me for information I'd previously promised to give her. The problem is, before I have a chance to get back to her something else typically comes in with an urgent deadline and I forget all about it. She's now taken to emailing me, which I resent – firstly, because I don't have time to read her lengthy emails, and secondly, because I think she's trying to catch me out."

Kao senses Karl is nearly in overwhelm. "Wow, that sounds like a lot going on! And if you were to name the issue in a nutshell, what would you say?"

Karl scratches his head and looks at Kao quizzically. "I don't know."

Kao tries a different question. "OK, and if a friend of yours was telling you what you've just told me, what would be your assessment of what's happening?"

"Ah, I get you. I'm not keeping in touch well. I'm not giving her what she needs or updating her when I say I will. And she is pushing me to honour my commitments. I definitely think it's a question of trust. Rebecca doesn't trust me and I'm beginning not to trust her." Relief floods through Karl's body as he finally starts to see the wood from the trees.

"Rebecca doesn't trust you and you are beginning to not trust her," Kao repeats back. "And is there anything else that would be useful for me to know?"

Karl hangs his head and frowns. "No, except that I'm noticing a deterioration in relationships with my other colleagues as well."

"And what would you like to have happen?" Kao asks.

Karl takes a moment to consider the question. "Well, I'd like them to trust me and for our relationships to be back to how they were six months ago."

Kao enquires gently, "And what's important to you about them trusting you?"

Karl's eyes moisten. "In the past, we've always worked well together and I feel sad that this is where we've got to. Being part of the team is really important to me – it's the most fulfilling part of the job and why I go to work."

Kao can see how much this means to Karl and wants him to feel empowered. "And what aspects of trust are within your control?"

"I was always taught that you have to give trust to receive it," Karl replies. "So, perhaps if I think about what would make me trust someone, I could do that for them, and that would start to increase the trust between me and my colleagues."

Kao smiles encouragingly. "That sounds like a plan. So, what would make you trust someone, Karl?"

Karl responds quickly. "Their personal credibility. Are they good at their job? Do they know their stuff? Can they deliver quality results in a timely manner?"

"And what else?" Kao enquires.

"Reliability. Do they do what they say they're going to do? Are they consistent? Is their word their bond? Do they keep in touch when they say they will?"

Kao probes further. "And what else?"

Karl continues, "Our levels of intimacy." They both laugh. "Not like that! How well I know the person. What is the quality of our relationship? What do we have in common? Do we have a connection? Is there a shared sense of purpose?"

Kao is tenacious with his questioning. "And what else would make you trust someone?"

Karl pauses in consideration. "There is something for me about their level of self-interest. Do they prioritise the interests of the team and the business, or are they focused on what is best for them? I'm also less likely to trust someone if I don't believe they genuinely care about me."

Again, Kao asks, "And is there anything else?"

Karl shakes his head. "Nope. I think that's about it in terms of things that determine whether I trust someone or not."

Kao is impressed. "It sounds to me like you've perfectly described Maister, Green and Galford's 'Trust Equation'[22] in their book *The Trusted Advisor*."

Karl says, "Oh yeah, didn't we learn about that together in our training network group?"

Kao nods. "Yes! OK, so here's the million-dollar question. In relation to the dynamic between you and Rebecca, what do you notice – and how would you rate yourself against the four criteria of self-interest, intimacy, credibility and reliability?"

Karl smiles to himself as the penny drops and he starts to feel more confident.

"In terms of self-interest, I think she knows I prioritise what is best for the team and genuinely have their best interests at heart. So, I think I'm doing OK with this one. I would have rated myself highly on intimacy in the past. We used to have a

---

22 For more information about the Trust Equation go to www.LisaBrice.co.uk/bquickcoachingresources.

pretty good relationship; we would have a laugh and a joke about things, and then crack on with the work. I imagine as the trust grows, this will naturally improve. I'd say credibility-wise, my score is not so hot now. I'd hope Rebecca still thinks I'm good at my job, although recently I've given her reason to doubt this, as I've not been keeping in touch or updating her about my progress. And of course, that impacts her and her workload. Reliability is where I would rate myself the lowest. I can see that she might experience me as being unreliable and I'd have to agree. She doesn't know where I'm at as I'm jumping from one project to another without any explanation or communication with her."

Kao captures what he has just heard. "Interesting. So you can see how Rebecca might experience you as unreliable?"

Karl lets out a sigh. "Yes. When I put myself in Rebecca's shoes, I can see how my behaviour must seem to her, and why she is struggling to trust me. I totally get it now and can understand how our relationship has deteriorated."

"What are you going to do about it?" Kao challenges gently.

Karl grins with relief. "First off, I'm going to ask for a chat and apologise to her. I want to explain my perception of the situation and ask her for her perspective. Then I'm hopeful that if we're both open-minded we can agree some new ways of working together that will improve team morale and productivity."

Kao is delighted for Karl, as he seems so much more positive than he did seven minutes ago. "Great. I've got to dash to my next session. Let's keep in touch, and you can tell me how it all works out."

Karl smiles. "Yes, that would be awesome. I could give you a call next Tuesday or Thursday evening?"

"Thursday is good for me, 7.30pm. How's that sound?" Kao responds.

"Good for me. Thanks so much, Kao. Hope you enjoy the rest

of the conference."

They both immediately take out their phones to put the appointment in their diaries, then turn and smile at each other.

Having listened to Karl's situation, Kao is even more determined to stick to his commitment to keep in touch with Karl. He really values their friendship and is grateful he managed to resurrect their relationship. He doesn't want to risk losing it by not keeping in touch.

Karl really values Kao's support and is appreciative of the opportunity to have a follow-up chat. He's realised the importance of taking a moment to diarise his appointments as they are agreed. Using his diary is a good first step to help him remember to keep in touch with people when he says he is going to.

Very soon it's Thursday evening, and Kao and Karl are catching up.

"So, my friend," Kao enquires, "how did your talk with Rebecca go?"

Karl seems really upbeat as he gives his update. "Pretty good, I have to say. We popped out for an early beer. I wanted to make our chat informal and I felt I owed her a drink at least. I started by apologising. Then I asked how she thought things were going between us, and what we could do to improve how we work together.

"We had a great chat and things have been so much better these last couple of days. We acknowledged that it was important to prioritise keeping in touch. We've scheduled a ten-minute catch-up each day, and if we don't need it we won't take it. I've promised Rebecca she will have my undivided attention in these catch-ups and I will prioritise giving her any updates she needs.

"Whilst the solution to this is, in part, putting some practical things in place to ensure we are communicating better, for me it is more about placing an importance on team relationships and prioritising our communication.

"I can be trustworthy. I need to invest in the relationship and communicate consistently and honestly. The only way we are going to be successful is by pulling together and working effectively as a team."

Kao is genuinely pleased for Karl. "I'm delighted for you. Let's keep in touch and have a beer together sometime soon!" Karl puts his phone down and smiles to himself. He has learnt a valuable lesson about the importance of keeping in touch. Trust is a prerequisite for any productive relationship, and keeping in touch in a timely manner helps to breed trust. He's realised that utilising technology can help him honour his commitments. All the ingredients of the 'Trust Equation' are positively impacted when we keep in touch.

Kao reflects on how powerful it was to ask a few questions, listen intently, and paraphrase back what someone has just said. This type of coaching-style conversation helps provide clarity and perspective, and can reduce overwhelm.

bQUICK® Wins:

Keep in Touch and Ensure You Aren't Seen as Untrustworthy

- Be reliable – keep in touch and do what you say you are going to do, when you say you are going to do it.

- Be credible – do your job to the best of your ability and be professional at all times.

- Focus on the quality of the intimacy within your relationships.

- Balance your self-interest with the interests of your team and the business.

Part Three:
Conclusion

The bQUICK® Coaching Model
Reviewed

Time has flown by. It's the team's monthly management meeting, and they're reporting back on their experience of using the bQUICK® Coaching Model.

Blaise kicks off the meeting. "I'm delighted to say I've noticed some great coaching-style conversations going on, not only with you and your team members, but also between some of you. Well done, everyone! I'd love to hear how you got on over the last couple of months using bQUICK® Coaching. And then I want to do a little exercise with you all. Who'd like to report back first?"

Queenie raises her hand and is quick to speak. "In general, I was surprised by how much better people responded to me when I used a questioning-style approach. My caveat is that sometimes people can't find their own answers and they just don't know what to do."

Blaise smiles encouragingly. "Absolutely, Queenie. Remember the Situational Leadership® Model we talked about at the Lunch and Learn session? Sometimes coaching isn't the most appropriate leadership intervention. Sometimes the person doesn't yet have the knowledge or skills to come up with their own solution. Coaching is just one of your options. Our aim is to choose a coaching-style conversation whenever we can."

Imogen speaks up next. "I've found, rather than telling people what to do, it's been more helpful to support them to find things out for themselves. I've discovered this has worked really well, even with new team members. As a result, I'm happy to say I've developed a new habit! When I'm asked about things I would previously have explained, now I ask questions like, 'What do you think could be a good way of you handling it?' or 'Who else could you find in the company that might have the information you need?' I've found that this encourages people to use their initiative and deepens their knowledge. And it's saved me loads of time! And of course I don't always do this; it depends on the person and the situation."

Blaise smiles to himself. He's pleased that Imogen has clearly embraced bQUICK® Coaching and is now empowering her team members to be responsible for their own learning. He goes on to prompt, "And what does anyone else want to share?"

Christina replies, "I love the model – it is so quick and easy to use."

Blaise looks around the room, making eye contact with everyone, checking if anyone else wants to feed back at this stage. "Before we move on to the review exercise, I'm curious to hear what else you want to do to become even more effective coaches and build on our successes so far."

Queenie raises her hand. "I'd like to learn more about Clean Language."

Christina says, "I'd like to go on the four-day coaching programme, the course Kao did."

Imogen nods in agreement. "And I would too, particularly as I love the idea of experiencing embodied leadership with the horses."

Ben joins in. "I'd really like to train to become a HeartMath® Certified Coach."

Blaise smiles at his team, delighted with their enthusiasm. "And what can we do collectively?"

Kao smiles. "I'd like to suggest that we all commit to continuing to practise using the bQUICK® Coaching Model for another two months. And let's agree to report back on the difference it is making for each of us and our teams at our next management meeting."

Udo nods in agreement and enthusiastically adds, "What about setting up a coaching circle between ourselves? I'm thinking this would give us an opportunity to practise using the bQUICK® Coaching Model in a different context, enabling us to see how well it also works during a series of longer, structured, and more formal coaching sessions."

Blaise grins. He's so proud of his team and how much they have benefited from experimenting with a new style of communication. To him, they feel like a high-performing team now.

"Great! Thanks, everyone, for your feedback. I'll pick up with you individually about how you can access the trainings you mentioned. And please let me know if there is anything else I can do to support you in embedding coaching in our organisation. Are you happy for us to move on to the exercise now?"

The team members nod their approval.

Blaise continues, "As you can see, I've put up some flipcharts around the room. Each one has its own question. Some people call this exercise an Around the World Café. My invitation is for you to work in pairs. I'll give you ten minutes to discuss and note your answers before moving you on to the next flipchart. Standing up and moving will encourage full body learning and help you tap into all your intelligence centres, not just those brilliant brains of yours."

As the team works together, Blaise is enjoying the buzz and energy that is in the room.

On the next few pages are the completed flipcharts.

WHAT DID I LEARN ABOUT MYSELF AS A COACH?

- I CAN JUST ASK QUESTIONS AND LISTEN
    - I'M NOT EXPECTED TO HAVE ALL THE ANSWERS!

- BUILDING RAPPORT IS CRITICAL

- I CAN MANAGE MY EMOTIONS AND BE PATIENT WITH PEOPLE

- MY ROLE, AS THE COACH, IS TO RAISE AWARENESS; IT IS THE OTHER PERSON'S RESPONSIBILITY TO CHANGE THEIR BEHAVIOUR

- IT'S HARD WORK TO KEEP MY ATTENTION ON THE HERE AND NOW, AND NOT LET MY MIND WANDER

- USING HUMOUR AND BEING A BIT PROVOCATIVE CAN SHIFT THE OTHER PERSON'S PERSPECTIVE

- STAY CURIOUS – LISTEN WITHOUT JUDGEMENT

Lisa Brice
Inspiring Excellence

WHAT ARE THE CHALLENGES OF USING bQUICK® COACHING?

- SOMETIMES PEOPLE JUST WANT ME TO TELL THEM THE ANSWER AND THEY GET ANNOYED WHEN I DON'T

- IT'S HARD TO COACH WELL WHEN I'M FRUSTRATED OR STRESSED

- SOMETIMES PEOPLE COME UP WITH SOLUTIONS TO PROBLEMS I DON'T AGREE WITH

- PEOPLE OFTEN FOCUS ON THE PROBLEM AND STRUGGLE TO ARTICULATE WHAT THEY WANT

- IT'S SO TEMPTING TO GIVE SOLUTIONS, ESPECIALLY WHEN I KNOW ABOUT THE SITUATION AND/OR TIME IS OF THE ESSENCE

- GETTING THE PERSON TO SAY WHAT THEY REALLY THINK INSTEAD OF WHAT THEY THINK I WANT TO HEAR

- COMING UP WITH GREAT QUESTIONS, WHILST STILL LISTENING FULLY TO WHAT THE COACHEE IS ACTUALLY SAYING

Lisa Brice
Inspiring Excellence

WHAT ARE THE BENEFITS OF USING bQUICK® COACHING?

- IT FREES UP MY TIME TO FOCUS ON THE IMPORTANT STUFF

- MY TEAM ARE MORE ENGAGED AND TEAM MORALE HAS IMPROVED

- IT CREATES INSIGHTS, ENHANCES PROBLEM SOLVING AND CREATIVITY

- ALLOWING PEOPLE TO COME UP WITH THEIR OWN SOLUTIONS HAS BUILT THEIR CONFIDENCE

- EXPLORING WHAT THE PERSON WANTS AND WHAT THE OUTCOME WILL DO FOR THEM INCREASES THEIR MOTIVATION AND COMMITMENT TO THE TASK IN HAND

- ASKING QUESTIONS, LISTENING AND PARAPHRASING CAN HELP REDUCE OVERWHELM AND PROVIDE CLARITY

- TEAM MEMBERS ARE USING THEIR OWN INITIATIVE, AND PERFORMANCE HAS INCREASED

Lisa Brice
Inspiring Excellence

After reviewing their answers, Blaise is feeling even more excited about the opportunities a coaching culture will bring to the business. He praises his team. "Great work, everyone! I'm delighted with how you've embraced having short, impactful, coaching-style conversations. And I can sense that you clearly recognise the benefits of coaching, rather than automatically telling someone what to do. You've proved how effective using the bQUICK® Coaching Model is and now know it is as easy as asking these six transformational questions:

- Am I present?
- What is happening now?
- What would you like to have happen?
- What could you do?
- What are you going to do?
- When shall we check back in?

It really is that simple!"

What's Next?

I hope you've found the insights into bQUICK® Coaching enjoyable and thought-provoking. Perhaps you're now eager to explore how these ideas can enrich your personal coaching approach.

There are numerous ways to delve deeper into this material. At the end of each chapter, you'll find links to complementary resources that expand on the concepts discussed by the characters in the book. You are welcome to download these. Please contact me if you have any questions. I'd love to hear your success stories using the bQUICK® Coaching model.

If you and your team are interested in honing the key skills that underpin this coaching style, I offer a range of in-house programmes, including half-day introduction masterclasses, one-day and two-day courses, designed to empower you to lead with a coaching style.

For those seeking a more comprehensive training experience, you might consider joining my 8-week online programme or attending my four-day NLP Diploma in Coaching.

If you've interested in exploring the concept of embodied leadership through interactions with horses to enhance your coaching stance, you could join one of my Horses for Courses® Programmes.

In response to a number of requests, I'm also offering a Train the Trainer Programme, which will give you the expertise and licensing permissions to use the book, model and masterclasses within your own business and with your clients.

Please email me for more information at Lisa@LisaBrice.co.uk or check out my website: www.LisaBrice.co.uk.

Resources

To find out more about any of the topics listed below that are referenced in this book, please scan the QR code or visit www.LisaBrice.co.uk/bquickcoachingresources.

The Business Case for Coaching
Situational Leadership® Model
The bQUICK® Coaching Model
Matching and Mirroring
Anchoring
HeartMath®
HeartMath Quick Coherence® Technique
Open Questions
Listening to Understand
Invitational Language
Clean Language
Unconscious Positive Intentions
Problem Thinking
Outcome Thinking
Embedded Commands
The PRO Model
Coaching with Horses and Horses for Courses®
The Advice Monster
The Drama Triangle
Future Pacing
Big and Small Chunk Thinking
Implementation Intentions
The Trust Equation

Acknowledgements

Being dyslexic, I've found writing this book, short though it is, really challenging at times. I've had to overcome a host of limiting beliefs about myself and my ability to communicate in the written form. In other words, this book has been a long time in the writing – and it would not have been possible without the help and support of some very special people.

I want to formally acknowledge and say a heartfelt thank you to all the people who have helped me, coached me, and given me feedback. I couldn't have done it without you.

Particularly, I'd like to thank Joe Rappaport for his endless patience and hours of help wordsmithing, and Alan Graham and Louise Gordon for the numerous coaching calls. Thanks also to my kind friends and colleagues, who have read the numerous draft versions; my wonderful clients, who have given me feedback about their experience of being coached through the bQUICK® Coaching Model; and, of course, all the trainers I have had the delight and privilege of learning from over the last three decades.

Finally, I'd like to thank Ellen Watts, my wonderful book coach, who has smiled and held my hand the whole way through the process.

And finally, finally, thank you to my wonderful husband Adam, for his continued love and devotion.

About Lisa Brice

International Trainer | Personal Performance Coach
Business Consultant | Equine Assisted Learning Specialist

Lisa Brice, a seasoned professional in the world of learning and development, describes herself as having an innate love of learning. For the last three decades she has dedicated her professional life to the pursuit of coaching excellence. With a global reach that extends beyond the United Kingdom, Lisa's passion is to facilitate insights and behavioural change. Her ultimate goal is to foster transformation and deliver tangible outcomes for her clients, their teams and their businesses.

Lisa draws on an extensive repertoire of developmental approaches to deliver a result-focused learning experience. She is a certified HeartMath® Coach and Trainer, NLP Master Trainer and Coach, Systemic Coaching & Constellations Practitioner and a pioneer in the field of Equine Assisted Learning. Her worldwide clientele benefits from this unique synthesis of profound wisdom and extensive experience.

Lisa and her team are renowned for their tailor-made outcome-focused training and coaching programmes. Their services cater to a wide spectrum of industries, corporate clients, SMEs and charitable organisations.

Clients who have experienced Lisa's training describe it as a one-of-a-kind, profoundly inspirational life-altering journey that surpasses all expectations – an invigorating breath of fresh air.

Lisa loves delivering open and in-house programmes from her beautiful converted barn in Northamptonshire. This immersive, relaxed training environment, Lisa explains, is conducive to full-body, experiential and brain-friendly learning.

The training room is a flexible space that can cater for a variety of formal or informal set-ups. The gardens and paddocks make great breakout areas and during the breaks delegates often go for a walk, either to visit the horses or the neighbouring alpacas.

Lisa believes that being away from the hustle and bustle of commercial life, and not in a formal hotel or conference centre, really helps her learners access their creativity and heightens their learning and retention.

Currently, Lisa offers a range of courses including NLP and coaching qualifications, in-house coaching and leadership development programmes, one-to-one personal performance coaching, and Equine Assisted Learning programmes.

When Lisa isn't training, speaking, coaching or writing books, she enjoys riding and caring for her beautiful horses, Badger and Wilson.

You can get in touch by emailing her at Lisa@LisaBrice.co.uk or check out her website at www.LisaBrice.co.uk.

Printed in Great Britain
by Amazon

42680170R00066